YOUNG PEOPLE'S MASS BOOK

YOUNG PEOPLE'S MASS BOOK

Harold Winstone
in collaboration with Sister Maria de la Cruz

With Suggestions for Mass in Schools

GEOFFREY CHAPMAN
LONDON DUBLIN MELBOURNE 1971

Geoffrey Chapman Ltd
18 High Street, Wimbledon, London SW 19

Geoffrey Chapman (Ireland) Ltd
5–7 Main Street, Blackrock, County Dublin

Illustrations by Etienne Morel, Alberto Garcia-Alvarez and the Benedictine nuns of Cockfosters.

The scriptural passages in this book have been simplified for use by children.

New English translations of the Order of Mass, copyright © 1969, the International Committee on English in the Liturgy, Inc. All rights reserved.

Texts of *Gloria*; *Holy, holy*; *Creed*; *Our Father*; *Dialogue before Preface*: approved by the Hierarchies of England, Wales, Scotland and Ireland in 1966.

Compilation © Geoffrey Chapman, 1970

First published 1970
ISBN 0 225 65757 0 *(paper binding)*
ISBN 0 225 65847 x *(de luxe binding)*

Concordat cum originali: John Humphreys, JCD
    Secretary to the National Liturgical Commission of England and Wales
Nihil obstat: Harold Winstone *Censor*
Imprimatur: † Victor Guazzelli, *Vic. Gen.*
Westminster, 22 October, 1970

Printed in Great Britain by
Lowe and Brydone (Printers) Ltd, London.

Contents

How to use this book 6
What the Mass is 9
Things needed for the celebration of Mass 12
How we offer Mass together 18
Some suggestions for a classroom Mass 20

PART ONE
The Order of Mass 23

PART TWO
Prayers, lessons and Gospels for various times of the year, and for various feasts 59

Index of seasons and feasts 160

How to use this book

One thing emerges clearly from the recent changes that have been authorized in the liturgy. It is that all the faithful are expected to take an active and vocal part in the Mass. Care has been taken to make every part of the Mass capable of achieving its proper purpose. The greeting must be a real greeting, the penitential act a genuine act of sorrow for sin, the Word of God must really speak to this community, God must become present to this community in his Word and in the sacrament.

So we now have an adult liturgy which is capable of fulfilling these demands. But what of our children? In recent years priests, parents, teachers and catechists have given much thought to the special needs of children in liturgical worship. They too must be able to take an active and intelligent part in the Mass. Children are not young adults, they exist in their own right. They have their own ways of feeling and thinking and reacting to the world outside them. We must provide them with a form of worship which makes sense to them and which truly expresses their own deeply felt religious needs. Their way of worship must be adapted to their age, their degree of understanding, their capacity for contributing actively to what is being done.

HOW TO USE THIS BOOK

This book makes no attempt to do this in detail, because no book can take account of every circumstance. The way in which Mass is celebrated in the spirit of the new liturgy must be dictated not by hard and fast rules such as those laid down in the rubrics of the Tridentine Missal, but by the very much more pastoral directives of the new Roman Missal which lay great emphasis on the actual pastoral situation in which the Mass is being offered. The people and their needs become the all-important consideration.

What this book attempts to do is to provide basic, simple texts which may serve as models for a children's liturgy, or at least be of some assistance to those responsible for the liturgy in children's groups. The children themselves should be as involved as possible in the preparation of their own worship. The decoration of the chapel or classroom, the making of altar-linen and vestments, the composition of prayers, especially bidding prayers, the choice of songs and readings, the musical accompaniment, the preparation of gifts to be offered at the altar, are all things in which the children can co-operate, so that the Mass really becomes their Mass. The Word of God may make a more immediate impact on small children through being acted out in the form of a simple play in which as many children as possible have parts (see the Passion Play for Good Friday).

As in all liturgy, the important thing is that whatever is done shall really express the deep concerns of all those taking part. This is not to deny the power of

HOW TO USE THIS BOOK

God to give grace through the sacramental action. It remains true, however, that the more genuine liturgy is in expressing the real dispositions and aspirations of those taking part, the more open will the individual be to receiving and responding to the grace of God.

This book may be found useful for children to use at Sunday Mass, especially in those parishes which provide a special children's Mass on Sundays. But it envisages mainly a school situation where Mass is said with the children on weekdays. It therefore provides a sufficient number of sample Masses for every week of the school year. It does not attempt to provide music for these Masses, as many suitable children's hymn books already exist for this purpose and it is assumed that by now most schools will be well equipped with these. Needless to say, hymns or songs should be chosen which suit the liturgical action they are intended to accompany, and which are in harmony with the theme of the particular Mass.

The test of a good liturgy is its capacity to bring happiness to those who take part in the celebration, a growing spirit of community, and a truly Christian approach to life.

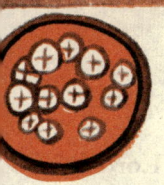  

What the Mass is

Everything that lives needs food. Plants and animals need food to keep them alive and make them grow.

Human beings need food too: that is why we gather round the family table at mealtimes.

But our physical life is not the only kind of life. God gave us a new life when we were baptized. He gave us the life of grace. This life also needs to grow, and therefore it needs food. Our Father in heaven gives us just the right sort of food for it, the best food he has: the body of his Son, Jesus Christ. This wonderful food is given to us at Mass.

At Mass, we gather round the altar with the priest and the whole parish. We do what our Saviour and his apostles did.

The evening before he died, Jesus and his apostles had a meal together. It was the Last Supper. During the meal, Jesus took some bread. He blessed it, broke it and gave it to his apostles, saying:

"Take this, all of you, and eat it:
this is my body."

Then he took the cup of wine, blessed it and gave it to his apostles, saying:

"Take this, all of you, and drink from it:
this is the cup of my blood,
The blood of the new and everlasting covenant.
It will be shed for you and for all men
so that sins may be forgiven.
Do this in memory of me."

WHAT THE MASS IS

When we celebrate Mass and receive our Lord's body, we are as near to Christ as the apostles were at the Last Supper.

The Last Supper happened on Holy Thursday.

The next day, Good Friday, Jesus was condemned to death. They made him carry his cross to Calvary, a hill near Jerusalem where criminals were put to death. There Jesus was nailed to a cross. The Son of God was nailed to a cross, as though he were just another criminal. For three hours he suffered agonies on the cross, sacrificing his life for our sins.

In the Mass, Christ offers in our midst the same sacrifice as he offered on the cross. St Paul says: "As often as you eat this bread and drink this cup, you are announcing the Lord's death until he comes again."

At Mass we think of our Saviour's sacrifice on the cross, and offer ourselves with him to the Father.

On Easter morning Jesus came out of his tomb alive. He had risen from the dead. His body was glorified, and shone with glorious majesty.

Jesus does not desert us.

He says: "Behold I am with you all through the days that are coming, until the end of the world." Christ our Lord is really with us, in our very midst.

When we come for Mass, he is here to celebrate it with us. And then what happened on Holy Thursday and Good Friday is renewed in our presence.

We all celebrate Mass together. That is why, when we pray at Mass, we use the word "we", not "I".

At Mass we watch what is going on and listen attentively. We join in the prayers and the singing.

We all offer Mass together and, if possible receive our Lord's body.
In Holy Communion we receive the body and blood of our Lord Jesus Christ as food. This food gives us strength in our journey through life. We too will one day rise again and live forever with God, with Christ and all his saints in our Father's kingdom.

Jesus says: "I am the living bread that came down from heaven. Whoever eats this bread will live for ever."

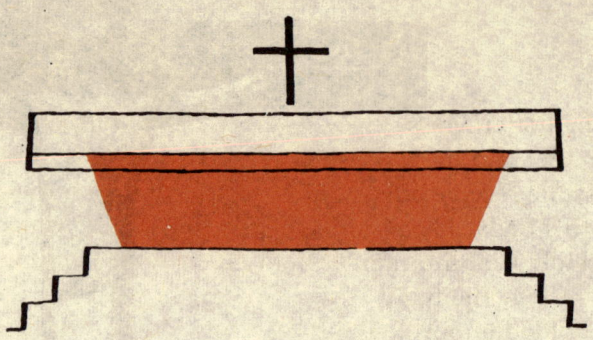

Things needed for for the Celebration of Mass

For the first part of the Mass
The Service of the Word of God

The President's Chair
This is where the priest sits when he is not leading the prayers, reading or preaching.

The Reading Desk, or Lectern
This may be covered with a piece of material called a Lectern Fall. This should be of the colour of the day (*see below*). On the Lectern is the *Lectionary*, or Book of Readings from the Bible.

For the second part of the Mass
The Eucharistic Sacrifice

The Altar
The holy sacrifice is celebrated on a kind of *table* called an altar. This contains the *relics* (the bodily

remains) of some holy martyrs, who let themselves be put to death rather than give up their faith in Christ. We keep their relics in the altar to remind us that they and all the saints are with us at Mass, for the Mass is the sacrifice of the whole Church, on earth and in heaven.

The altar is covered with white cloths. On or near the altar are a crucifix and candles.

On the altar steps is a *bell,* which may be rung at the principal parts of the Mass, to attract our attention and to express our joy in Christ's coming.

The Gifts

The gifts, which are brought to the altar and changed during the Mass into our Lord's body and blood, are unleavened *bread* (hosts) and pure *wine* made from grapes.

The Vessels

For the bread there is a plate made of some valuable material. It is called a *paten.*

For the wine there is a wine-cup, or *chalice.*

Small hosts may be kept in a container shaped rather like a chalice and called a *ciborium.*

At the beginning of Mass the wine is on a table at the side of the altar, in a tiny jug called a *cruet.* Another cruet contains water.

A drop of water is mixed with the wine at the Offertory, when the priest prepares the gifts for the sacrifice.

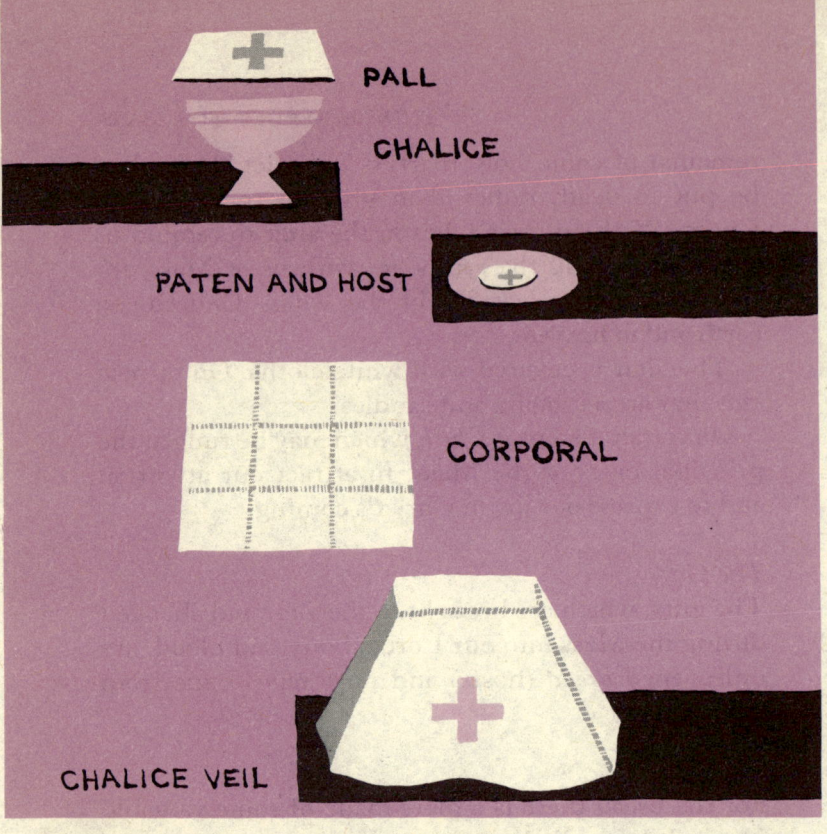

Water is also used to wash the priest's hands and the chalice.

The Chalice and its Covering
A linen cloth, folded in three lengthwise, is put over the chalice. This cloth is called a *purificator*; the priest uses it for drying the chalice.

The *paten*, with the host, is put on the purificator.

On the paten is a square piece of stiff linen called a *pall*, which is used as a cover for the chalice during the Mass.

THINGS NEEDED FOR MASS

From the Offertory until after the Communion, the chalice stands on a linen cloth called a *corporal*.

The *chalice veil* is draped over the chalice.

The Priest's Vestments

At Mass, the priest wears the following vestments:

the *amice*, a linen shoulder-cloth;

the *alb*, a long, white tunic;

the *girdle*, or cincture, which gathers in the alb round the waist;

the *stole*, a long strip of material which the priest at Mass wears round the neck and hanging down in front.

the *chasuble*, worn over the other vestments.

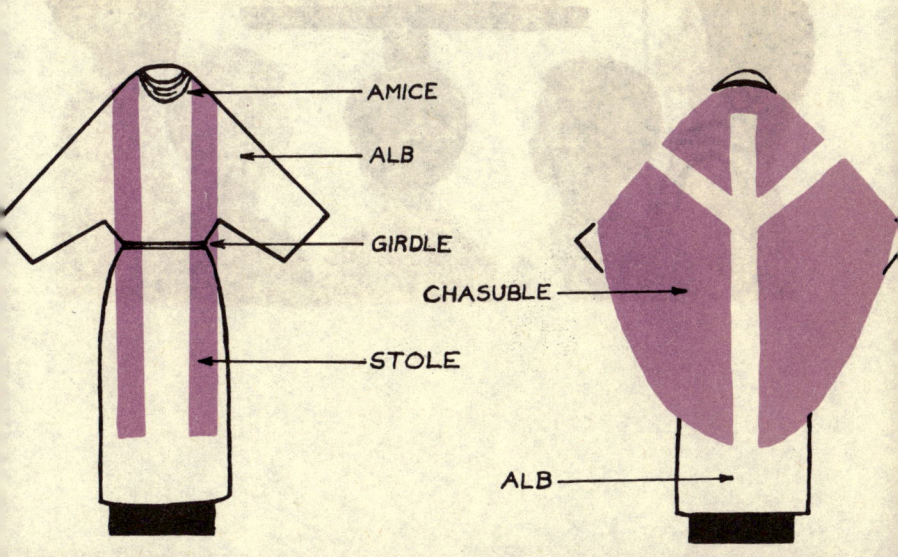

THINGS NEEDED FOR MASS

The Missal
This is a large book which contains the prayers and chants of the Mass. It is sometimes published in three parts: a *Book of Collects* for use at the President's chair; a *Sacramentary* for use at the altar. A *Lectionary* containing the readings from scripture, is used at the lectern.

THINGS NEEDED FOR MASS

The Colours

The colour of the vestments and of the chalice depends on the feast or the season of the Church's year.

White is a sign of joy and purity. It is used at Christmas, Easter, and other feasts of our Lord. It is also used on the feasts of our Lady, and of the angels, confessors and virgins.

Red is the colour of fire and blood. It is used in Masses of the Holy Spirit, on the feasts of the apostles and martyrs, and on Good Friday.

Purple is the penitential colour, and is used during Advent and Lent. It may also be used instead of black as the colour of mourning at Masses for the Dead.

Rose-coloured vestments may be used on the third Sunday of Advent and the Fourth Sunday of Lent.

Green, a colour which symbolizes hope, is used on the Sundays after Epiphany and after Pentecost. This is because Sunday is a special day for keeping alive our hope in the resurrection.

Black, the colour of mourning, may be used at Masses for the Dead.

How we offer Mass together

We all offer Mass together. Everyone has something to do, something to say, and something to sing. The Mass is not just something which the priest does and which we watch.

The Priest says the official prayers of the Church: the Opening Prayer, Prayer over the Offerings, and Postcommunion prayer. He also reads the Gospel (unless he has a deacon to assist him). But most important of all he says the great Eucharistic Prayer, during which our offerings of bread and wine are changed into the body and blood of Christ.

A Reader from among the people reads the Lessons and the Bidding Prayers or Prayers of Petition.

We All sing the hymns, answer the prayers, present our gifts at the altar, and come to the altar to receive Communion.

The Servers lead the people in their prayers and responses, bring the wine and water to the priest, and ring the bell. Before Mass they prepare the altar and light the candles. They may carry these to the altar at the entrance procession at the beginning of Mass. After Mass they put out the candles and help the priest to clear away. Thus the server helps both the priest and the people.

HOW WE OFFER MASS TOGETHER

At different times during the Mass we stand, kneel and sit.

Standing reminds us of our Lord's resurrection, his triumph over death. We always stand when we pray together, recognizing Christ's presence among us.

Kneeling is an attitude of worship. It is also a sign of repentance.

We *sit down* to listen to the Epistle, to chants sung by the choir, and to the sermon.

We *stand* for the Gospel, out of reverence for God's word.

The church is God's house, where his people gather to worship. We observe silence and quiet there, unless we are singing or praying together. We respect the recollection of people who want to think, to pray in silence, who need peace and quiet in the midst of their worries and sufferings.

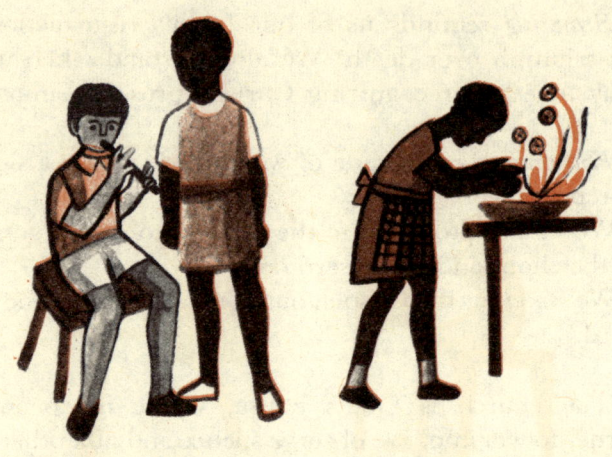

Some suggestions for a classroom Mass

1. The children help in preparing the classroom, decorating it with pictures and flowers, erecting the altar and lectern, even making the candlesticks, crucifix, bookstand, etc.

2. The hymns, readings and prayers (especially the Bidding Prayers or Prayers of Petition) are well-prepared beforehand. If possible, a group of children learns to accompany the singing on recorders, glockenspiel, etc. As much of their ordinary classwork as possible should be made to centre round the Mass, so that the children learn to think of the Mass as an integral part of their life.

SUGGESTIONS FOR A CLASSROOM MASS

3. All the children may bring their gifts to the altar at the Offertory. They can bring their best work, a project they have worked on together, cakes they have baked, their needlework, pottery, or their pennies and toys collected for charities that interest them.

Alternatively, they can come and put their host in the ciborium. As they do so they may say their name, so that they understand that the bread represents themselves. Added point is thus given to the words of the priest when he gives them Communion: "The Body of Christ."

4. The teacher is the best judge of what the children can do with a natural ease, and with understanding and profit. The keynote of the celebration should always be joy, even in a penitential season. The priest should do all he can to identify himself with the children and not be too formal or aloof. Needless to say, Mass should always be said facing the children.

PART ONE

The Order of Mass

I

The Introductory Rites

The Entrance

A suitable hymn should be sung while the priest and servers go to the altar.
Suggested texts for singing or reciting:

Advent
Never cease rejoicing!
Rejoice, for your Saviour is coming.
Show us, Lord, how we can serve you.

The Christmas Season and Epiphany
A child has been born for us;
a Son has been given to us.
He bears on his shoulders
the sceptre of God's kingdom.
Sing to the Lord a song that is new,
for he has done wonderful things for us.

Lent and Passiontide
You have mercy, O God,
on all your creatures.
You forgive us our sins,
for you are our God,
the Lord who loves us.

ENTRANCE SONG

The Easter Season
Christ has truly risen from the dead, alleluia.
Our king and conqueror,
we need you more than we can say.

Pentecost
The Spirit of the Lord fills all the earth, alleluia.
The whole universe has learned to understand his voice.
O Lord, my God,
how wonderful is your name the wide world over.

Sundays after Pentecost
I am the Saviour of my people, says the Lord.
Whatever your trouble, call out to me and I will hear you.
My eyes are fixed on you, my God.

Feasts of our Lord
At the name of Jesus
everyone in heaven and earth must kneel and say,
Christ is the Lord.
Praise the Lord.
Serve the Lord with joy.

Feasts of our Lady
We greet you, holy mother.
You gave birth to the king of heaven and earth.
Jesus said:
See, mother, there is your son.
To his disciple he said:
See, there is your mother.

Feasts of Apostles
O God, how highly you have honoured your friends.
How wonderful it is to praise you
and to spread your fame abroad.

Feasts of Martyrs
The martyr is glad
because of the strength his Saviour gives him.
All his trust is in God.
What cause have we to be afraid?

Feasts of Saints
The saint is one who thinks always of God
and speaks his truth.
How wonderful it is to be a witness for the Lord.

Feasts of Holy Women
You have loved right and hated wrong.
That is why God has given you such joy.

Then the priest says:

Priest   In the name of the Father, and of the Son, and of the Holy Spirit.
Children **Amen.**

P.   The grace and peace of God our Father and the Lord Jesus Christ be with you.
C.   **Amen.**

P.   My brothers and sisters,* to prepare ourselves to celebrate the sacred mysteries, let us call to mind our sins.

Or, My dear children.

I CONFESS

After a brief silence, the priest says:

(*P.* Let us make our confession together:)
All **I confess to almighty God,**
and to you, my brother and sisters,
that I have sinned through my own fault

We strike our breast and continue:

in my thoughts and in my words,
in what I have done,
and in what I have failed to do;
and I ask blessed Mary, ever virgin,
all the angels and saints,
and you, my brothers and sisters,
to pray for me to the Lord our God.

The priest says the absolution:

May almighty God have mercy on us,
forgive us our sins,
and bring us to everlasting life.
C. **Amen.**

A plea for mercy

This may be said or sung.
We call upon Jesus to take pity on us, and on all who suffer in the world.

P. Lord, have mercy.
C. **Lord, have mercy.**
P. Christ, have mercy.
C. **Christ, have mercy.**
P. Lord, have mercy.
C. **Lord, have mercy.**

GLORIA

The Gloria

If the Gloria is to be used, the priest begins, and everyone continues.
The Gloria may be said or sung.
We join with the whole of creation in blessing and praising God and Christ who leads us to God.

P. Glory be to God on high
All **And on earth peace to men who are God's friends.**
We praise thee.
We bless thee.
We adore thee.
We glorify thee.
We give thee thanks for thy great glory.
Lord God, heavenly King, God the almighty Father.
Lord Jesus Christ, only-begotten Son.
Lord God, Lamb of God, Son of the Father.
Thou who takest away the sins of the world, have mercy on us.
Thou who takest away the sins of the world, receive our prayer.
Thou who art seated at the right hand of the Father, have mercy on us.
For thou alone art the Holy One.
Thou alone art the Lord.
Thou alone art the Most High, Jesus Christ,
With the Holy Spirit; in the glory of God the Father. Amen.

OPENING PRAYERS

Opening prayer

P. Let us pray.

Silently we pray to thank God for his goodness to us, and ask for what we want him to give us in this Holy Mass.
Each Mass has its own special opening prayer.
We end the prayer by telling God the Father that we make our request in the name of his Son, Jesus Christ. The priest says:

P. We make our prayer through our Lord Jesus Christ, your Son, who lives and reigns with you and the Holy Spirit, one God, for ever and ever.

C. **Amen.**

We may pray like this:

In thanksgiving
O God, there is no end to your mercy,
no limit to your kindness;
we thank you for all your gifts.

For the grace to love God
O God, if we love you sincerely,
whatever happens to us will be for our good.
Give us the grace to love you so much that no kind of temptation will ever be able to separate us from you.

OPENING PRAYERS

For peace
O God, you are the source of all our holy desires,
all our right decisions,
and all our good actions.
Make us obedient to your commandments,
that we may spend our days in peace under your
  strong protection.

In times of sorrow and distress
Lord, show us your mercy and kindness.
Forgive us our sins,
and spare us the punishments they have deserved.

For our families
O God, listen to the prayers of Mary,
the virgin mother of our Lord Jesus Christ
and our mother too;
bless our family,
keeping it safe from all harm and all dangers.

For the sick
O God, you are the health and strength of your people;
it is for the sick that we are praying.
Heal their sickness,
that they may join us and the whole Church
in praising and thanking you.

OPENING PRAYERS

For the dead
Give, Lord, eternal rest to those who have died;
let them enjoy for ever the radiance of your light.
Give them never-ending happiness,
and grant that we too may one day share with them
the happiness of the saints in heaven.

For forgiveness
We have sinned, Lord,
but do not punish us as we deserve.
Forgive us and give us your peace.

For the spread of the faith
O God, it is your will that all men
should come to know the truth and be saved.
Send out apostles to herald the good news of salvation,
so that all nations may come to know you
and your Son, Jesus Christ our Lord.

II
The Service of the Word of God

We listen to the Word of God

The lesson is now read from the Bible, by the reader. We sit and listen to the Word of God. He begins with the words:

A reading from . . .

Through his prophets and apostles God tells us what we must believe and what Christ expects of us. We listen attentively. At the end of each reading, the reader says:

R. This is the Word of the Lord.
C. **Thanks be to God.**

Response and Alleluia

If there are two readings, a psalm is sung or said after the first one, and the Alleluia comes after the second one.
The Alleluia is a song of welcome to Christ who is going to speak to us in the Gospel.

The Gospel

The priest prays silently, asking God to make him worthy to read the Gospel. He then goes to the book and says:

P. The Lord be with you.
C. **And also with you.**
P. A reading from the holy gospel according to . . .

(Here the priest mentions the name of the evangelist: Matthew, Mark, Luke or John.)

C. **Glory to you, Lord.**

GOSPEL AND SERMON

We stand up and listen to the Gospel with great reverence. God is speaking to us through his Son.
The word Gospel means "good news".
The priest traces a small cross with his thumb over the first words of the Gospel. He then makes a similar cross on his forehead, mouth and heart. We should do the same, to show that we wish to think about Christ, speak about him, and love him with all our heart.
When he has finished reading the Gospel the priest says:

P.   This is the gospel of the Lord.

We answer:

C.   **Praise to you, Lord Jesus Christ.**

The priest reverently kisses the book, for it contains Christ's message. He prays silently:

P.   May the words of the gospel wipe away our sins.

The Sermon

After the gospel comes the sermon or homily. We listen attentively, for Christ speaks to us through his priests. He said: "Those who listen to you are listening to me." The priest helps us to understand what God's words mean. He tells us what Jesus has done for us, and what we should do, and can do, for Jesus.

The Creed

On Sundays and some feast days the Creed *(I believe) follows the sermon. In the Creed we tell God we believe everything he has taught us about himself and about what he has done for us.*

P. I believe in one God.

All **The almighty Father, maker of heaven and earth,**
Maker of all things, visible and invisible.
I believe in one Lord, Jesus Christ,
The only-begotten Son of God,
Born of the Father before time began,
God from God, Light from Light, true God from true God;
Begotten, not made, one in substance with the Father;
And through him all things were made.
For us men and for our salvation he came down from heaven,

(All bow, up to the words: was made man.)

Was incarnate of the virgin Mary by the power of the Holy Spirit, and was made man.
For our sake, too, under Pontius Pilate, he was crucified, suffered death, and was buried.
The third day he rose from the dead, as the scriptures had foretold.
He ascended to heaven, where he is seated at the right hand of the Father.
He will come again in glory to judge the living and the dead, and his kingdom will have no end.

CREED

I believe in the Holy Spirit, the Lord, the giver of life, who proceeds from the Father and the Son.
Together with the Father and the Son he is adored and glorified;
He it was who spoke through the prophets.
I believe in one, holy, catholic, and apostolic church.
I profess one baptism for the remission of sins.
And I look forward to the resurrection of the dead, and the life of the world to come. Amen.

PRAYER OF THE FAITHFUL

The Prayer of the Faithful

P. God our Father has called us here together as his family. Let us now ask him for everything that we need.

We may make up our own prayers, instead of the ones printed here.

Reader : Let us ask God to bless our Pope, our bishop and our priests.
Lord, hear us.
C. **Lord, graciously hear us.**
R. Let us ask God to bless our homes, and look after our mother and father, our sisters and brothers and all who come to visit us.
Lord, hear us.
C. **Lord, graciously hear us.**
R. Let us ask God to bless our school, our teachers and all who work for us.
Lord, hear us.
C. **Lord, graciously hear us.**
R. Let us ask God to bless all sick children and all poor children, especially those who cannot get enough to eat and those who have no friends and no toys to play with.
Lord, hear us.
C. **Lord, graciously hear us.**

R. Let us ask Mary, the mother of Jesus, to pray for us; she is our mother too.
C. **Hail Mary, full of grace,
the Lord is with thee.
Blessed art thou among women
and blessed is the fruit of thy womb, Jesus.
Holy Mary, mother of God,
pray for us sinners
now and at the hour of our death.
Amen.**
R. Let us now pray for a while in silence.

P. Heavenly Father, hear the prayers of your children and in your kindness give them all they ask. We ask you this through Jesus Christ our Lord.
C. **Amen.**

III
The Liturgy of the Eucharist

The presentation of the gifts

We now bring bread and wine to the altar and sing an Offertory song. The bread and wine stand for everything that we have and everything that we are.

When we give God a gift it is a sign that we want to give him our whole selves.

The priest lifts up the paten with the bread on it, and, quietly or aloud, blesses God for his gift.

P. Blessed are you, Lord, God of all creation.
 Through your goodness we have this bread to offer,
 which earth has given and human hands have made.
 It will become for us the bread of life.

C. **Blessed be God for ever.**

The priest pours wine and a little water into the cup, saying quietly:

P. By the mystery of this water and wine
 may we come to share in the divinity of Christ,
 who humbled himself to share in our humanity.

Then he takes the cup and raises it a little above the altar, saying quietly or aloud:

P. Blessed are you, Lord, God of all creation.
 Through your goodness we have this wine to offer,
 fruit of the vine and work of human hands.
 It will become our spiritual drink.

C. **Blessed be God for ever.**

PRESENTATION OF THE GIFTS

Having prepared the gifts, the priest washes his hands. Our hearts, too, must be clean if we want to share in offering this holy sacrifice.

P. Lord, wash away my iniquity;
cleanse me from my sin.

The priest stretches out his arms and says to us:

P. Pray, brethren, that our sacrifice
may be acceptable to God, the almighty Father.

C. **May the Lord accept the sacrifice at your hands,
for the praise and glory of his name,
for our good, and the good of all his Church.**

The priest gathers up all our prayers into a single prayer called the Prayer over the Gifts. *There is a different one for every feast and season.*

Lord, we have offered you our gifts;
make them holy, and make us holy too.
We ask you this through Christ our Lord. Amen.

The Eucharistic Prayer

Now begins the great prayer of praise, thanksgiving and offering called the prayer of consecration, or the Eucharistic Prayer.
It will include the words of consecration spoken by Jesus at the Last Supper.
The priest begins by telling us to raise up our hearts in gratitude to God.

P.   The Lord be with you.
C.   **And also with you.**
P.   Let us lift up our hearts.
C.   **We have raised them up to the Lord.**
P.   Let us give thanks to the Lord our God.
C.   **It is right and fitting.**

The priest sings or recites the Preface *with outstretched arms.*
The Preface may vary with the season of the year.

P.   Father, it is our duty and our salvation,
     always and everywhere
     to give you thanks
     through your beloved Son, Jesus Christ.
     He is the Word through whom you made the universe,
     the Saviour you sent to redeem us.
     By the power of the Holy Spirit
     he took flesh and was born of the Virgin Mary.
     For our sake he opened his arms on the cross;
     he put an end to death
     and revealed the resurrection.
     In this he fulfilled your will
     and won for you a holy people.

EUCHARISTIC PRAYER

    And so we join the angels and the saints
    in proclaiming your glory
    as we sing (say):
All **Holy, holy, holy, Lord God of hosts.**
Thy glory fills all heaven and earth.
Hosanna in the highest.
Blessed is he who comes in the name of the Lord.
Hosanna in the highest.

C.   Lord, you are holy indeed,
    the fountain of all holiness.
    Let your Spirit come upon these gifts to make them holy,
    so that they may become for us
    the body and blood of our Lord, Jesus Christ.

The Lord's supper

    Before he was given up to death,
    a death he freely accepted,
    he took bread and gave you thanks.
    He broke the bread,
    gave it to his disciples, and said:
    Take this, all of you, and eat it:
    this is my body which will be given up for you.

When supper was ended, he took the cup.
Again he gave you thanks and praise,
gave the cup to his disciples, and said:
**Take this, all of you, and drink from it:
this is the cup of my blood,
the blood of the new and everlasting
　covenant.
It will be shed for you and for all men
so that sins may be forgiven.
Do this in memory of me.**

Memorial acclamation of the people
Let us proclaim the mystery of faith:
1. **Christ has died,
   Christ is risen,
   Christ will come again.**
2. **Dying you destroyed our death,
   rising you restored our life.
   Lord Jesus, come in glory.**
3. **When we eat this bread and drink this
   　cup,
   we proclaim your death, Lord Jesus,
   until you come in glory.**
4. **Lord, by your cross and resurrection
   you have set us free.
   You are the Saviour of the world.**

EUCHARISTIC PRAYER

The memorial prayer

P. In memory of his death and resurrection,
we offer you, Father, this life-giving bread,
this saving cup.
We thank you for counting us worthy
to stand in your presence and serve you.

Invocation of the Holy Spirit

May all of us who share in the body and blood
  of Christ
be brought together in unity by the Holy Spirit.

Intercessions for the Church

Lord, remember your Church throughout the world;
make us grow in love,
together with N. our Pope,
N. our bishop, and all the clergy.

For the dead

Remember our brothers and sisters
who have gone to their rest
in the hope of rising again;
bring them and all the departed
into the light of your presence.

In communion with the saints

Have mercy on us all;
make us worthy to share eternal life
with Mary, the virgin mother of God,

with the apostles,
and with all the saints who have done your will
   throughout the ages.
May we praise you in union with them,
and give you glory
through your Son, Jesus Christ.

Concluding doxology

Through him,
with him,
in him,
in the unity of the Holy Spirit,
all glory and honour is yours,
almighty Father,
for ever and ever.
C. **Amen.**

COMMUNION

The Communion

The eucharistic prayer is now ended and we prepare to receive the body of our Lord in holy communion. We recite together Our Father, *the prayer of God's children.*

P. Let us pray with confidence to the Father
in the words our Saviour gave us:

All **Our Father, who art in heaven,
hallowed be thy name.
Thy kingdom come.
Thy will be done on earth, as it is in heaven.
Give us this day our daily bread,
and forgive us our trespasses,
as we forgive those who trespass against us,
and lead us not into temptation,
but deliver us from evil.**

P. Deliver us, Lord, from every evil,
and grant us peace in our day.
In your mercy keep us free from sin
and protect us from all anxiety
as we wait in joyful hope
for the coming of our Saviour, Jesus Christ.

All **For the kingdom, the power, and the glory are yours,
now and for ever.**

P. Lord Jesus Christ, you said to your apostles:
I leave you peace, my peace I give you.
Look not on our sins, but on the faith of your Church,
and grant us the peace and unity of your kingdom
where you live for ever and ever.

C. **Amen.**

COMMUNION

P. The peace of the Lord be with you always.
C. **And also with you.**

Then the priest may add:

P. Let us offer each other the sign of peace.

All make a sign of peace, according to local custom.
While the priest breaks the host we sing to Christ, the Lamb of God.
(In olden days, lambs used to be sacrificed to God. Our sacrificial lamb is Jesus Christ, the Lord.)

Agnus Dei

All **Lamb of God, you take away the sins of the world:**
have mercy on us.
Lamb of God, you take away the sins of the world:
have mercy on us.
Lamb of God, you take away the sins of the world:
grant us peace.

COMMUNION

The priest prepares to receive communion.
We too should prepare ourselves by asking God to help us to receive Jesus in communion with love.
Pray to God from your heart. If you cannot think of anything to say, say one or two of the following prayers.

You love me, Lord, and I love you.
You are calling me, and I am ready.
You invite me to your heavenly banquet.

The food that you give me is your own holy body.
You give me this food that I may live for ever.

Jesus, great God,
Jesus, good Shepherd.
I want to be with you always.

My Lord, I believe in you, I love you.

The priest shows us the sacred host and says:

P. This is the Lamb of God
who takes away the sins of the world.
Happy are those who are called to his supper.

All **Lord, I am not worthy to receive you,
but only say the word and I shall be healed.**

We all sing:

The Communion Song

We go to receive communion. As the priest gives us the host, he says:

P. The body of Christ.

We answer:

C. **Amen.**

After receiving Jesus as our holy food, there is a period of silence and we thank God for his great gift.
The following prayers will help you to express your love. Say them slowly.

Stay with me, Lord.
I want to become like you.
I want to please you always.
I want to love everyone for your sake,
because we are all united in you.

Jesus, you said, "I am the vine and you are the
 branches."
We will bear fruit,
so long as we remain in you.
We show our love for you
by keeping your commandments.
Bring all men to know you and love you.

Jesus, help all men to love you.
May your kingdom come.
Your life comes from the Father;
our life comes from you.
Lord, show us the Father.
Lead us into your glorious kingdom.

PRAYERS AFTER COMMUNION

The priest sings or says the Prayer after Communion—*a prayer of thanksgiving to God for the gift we have received. It varies with the feast. We pray that we may grow more like Jesus from sharing in this great sacrifice.*

P. Let us pray.
At the end of the prayer, the priest says:

P. We ask you this through Christ our Lord.
C. **Amen.**
We may pray like this:

Advent
Lord, we have received your holy gifts,
and now we pray that this heavenly food
may strengthen us against sin,
and prepare us for Christmas.

The Christmas Season and Epiphany
Great indeed is our joy
in celebrating the birthday of our Lord Jesus Christ.
He came to save us and to make us God's children.
May we always live as God's children.

Lent and Passiontide
Lord, this holy food that we have eaten gives us new life.
May it cleanse us from all our sins
and strengthen us.

The Easter Season
Almighty God, by this holy communion
you have given us the gift of new life.
May we always cherish this gift
and look after it well.

Pentecost
May the Holy Spirit come to us in this heavenly food
and make our hearts sinless and new.

Sundays after Pentecost
Lord, we have tasted the food of everlasting life.
We have taken it on our tongue;
may we welcome it in our hearts.

Feasts of our Lord
Almighty, everlasting God,
may the heavenly food we have received in holy
    communion make us truly holy.
May we live from now on as real Christians,
full of grace and joy.

Feasts of our Lady
You sent an angel, Lord,
to announce to us the birth of your Son, Jesus Christ.
Send now your grace into our hearts,
so that, by his passion and cross,
we may be brought to the glory of his resurrection.

PRAYERS AFTER COMMUNION

Feasts of Apostles
We have received, Lord, the bread of life.
We now unite our prayers with those of your holy
  apostle:
may the feast that we celebrate in his honour
help us on our road to heaven.

Feasts of Martyrs
Lord, we join with your holy martyr
in praying that this heavenly food we have taken
  on his feastday
may make us always pure in heart.

Feasts of Confessors
Lord, you have strengthened us with heavenly food.
May the prayers of your saint help us,
so that one day we may share with him the glory of
  heaven.

Feasts of Holy Women
Lord, you have given us all that our hearts could wish
  for.
May the prayers of this saint whose feast we are
  keeping
give us strength and joy.

DISMISSAL

The dismissal

The priest now sends us out into the world, as Jesus sent his apostles out into the world to continue his work. But first he says:

P. The Lord be with you.
C. **And also with you.**
P. May almighty God bless you, the Father, and the Son, and the Holy Spirit.
C. **Amen.**
P. Go in peace to love and serve the Lord.
C. **Thanks be to God.**

We all sing a hymn as the priest and the servers leave the altar.

PART TWO

**Prayers, Lessons and Gospels
for
Various Times of the Year
and for
Various Feasts**

First Week of Advent

Prayer

O God, all men once longed for a redeemer; they cried out to you to send them someone to save them. We too cry out in longing: Come, send us the redeemer to rescue us from our sins. Make our hearts ready to welcome him.

Lesson

from St Paul's letter to.the Romans

Brothers and sisters, it is time for us to wake up from sleep, for our Saviour is close at hand. The night is nearly over; day draws near. Let us then abandon the ways of darkness, and put on the armour of light. We want to be children of the light. We want to avoid sin and love Jesus.

Gospel

according to St Luke

In those days the angel Gabriel was sent by God to a maiden whose name was Mary. He said to her: "Hail, Mary, full of grace, the Lord is with thee." On hearing these words she was greatly disturbed, but the angel said to her: "Do not be afraid, Mary. You have found favour in the sight of God. You are to give birth to a son, and call him Jesus. He shall be great, and men will know him for the Son of God, the Most High. He shall reign for ever; his kingdom shall never have an end." The maiden replied: "Behold the handmaid of the Lord; let it be done to me according to your word."

Second Week of Advent

Prayer

O God, our Father, stir up in us the love of Jesus Christ your Son, so that we may prepare ourselves well for his coming. He lives and reigns with you and the Holy Spirit, one God, for ever and ever.

Lesson

from St Paul's letter to the Romans

Brothers and sisters: God never lets us down; he is always ready to give a helping hand. May he make us do the same, so that we can live together in peace, as good Christians should, and together sing the praises of the God and Father of our Lord Jesus Christ.

Welcome one another with open arms, as Christ has welcomed you, for the glory of God. May God reward your faith and fill you with peace and joy.

Gospel

according to St Matthew

At that time John the Baptist was preaching in the desert of Judea. "Repent," he said, "for the kingdom of heaven is at hand." John the Baptist was the person Isaiah was talking about when he said: "Someone in the desert is crying aloud, 'Prepare the way of the Lord, make his paths straight'."

Now John was dressed in camel's hair and he had a leather strap around his waist. He ate locusts and wild honey. Everyone in Jerusalem and Judea and the places near the River Jordan went out to hear him preach. They confessed their sins and were baptized by him in the river.

Third Week of Advent

Prayer

Come, Lord Jesus; help us to understand how much God loves us and what he has done for us through you, who live and reign with the Father and the Holy Spirit, one God for ever and ever.

THIRD WEEK OF ADVENT

Lesson

from the Book of Isaiah, the prophet

These are the words of the Lord: A child will be born of David's family, and the Spirit of the Lord will rest upon him: the spirit of good counsel and of strength, the spirit of knowledge and the fear of the Lord. He will not judge by appearances or by hearsay, but he will judge people as they really are and will help the poor and the down-trodden.

Gospel

according to St Luke

At that time John the Baptist said to the crowds of people who came to be baptized: "You brood of vipers! If you want to escape punishment you must repent and change your lives. It is no use saying 'We are the children of Abraham!' That will not save you, for God, if he likes, can make children of Abraham even out of these stones."

"What must we do, then?" they asked.

"You must share what you have with the poor," he said. "If you have two coats, give one of them away to someone who has no coat. If you have food, share it with people who have no food."

Fourth Week of Advent

Prayer

Put forth your power, Lord, and come. Save us from wickedness and every kind of evil. We pray to you with all our heart, for you live and reign with the Father and the Holy Spirit, one God, for ever and ever.

Lesson

from the Book of Isaiah, the prophet

You people of Jerusalem, go up to the top of a high mountain and tell the good news to the cities of Judah. Say to them: "The Lord your God is coming with great power. He is coming as a shepherd to lead his flock and gather the lambs in his arms."

Gospel

according to St Luke

In those days Mary arose and went with haste into the hill country, to a city of Judah. She went to the house of Zechariah and greeted Elizabeth. When Elizabeth heard Mary's greeting, the babe leaped in her womb and she was filled with the Holy Spirit. "Blessed are you among women," she cried, "and blessed is the fruit of your womb. How fortunate I am that the mother of my Lord should come to me. When I heard your greeting, the babe in my womb leaped for joy. How happy you are: you believed what the angel of the Lord told you."

Christmas

Midnight Mass

Prayer

O God, by the birth of Jesus you have made this most sacred night shine with the radiance of true light; for Jesus is the light of the world. May his light never leave us in this world so that in heaven we may share in the joys which he gives to those who love him.

Lesson

from St Paul's letter to Titus

Dear friend, the grace of God, our Saviour, has dawned on all men alike. It teaches us to live pure, upright and holy lives. We are looking forward to the day when Jesus Christ, our great God and Saviour, will come back again in glory. He gave himself to us once and he will rescue us from every evil. He wants his people to be holy and without sin. He wants them to belong to him, and to do good in this world. That is the lesson you must learn. That is the lesson you must preach to others.

Gospel

according to St Luke

In those days the Roman Emperor Augustus ordered that a list be made of all his subjects. Everyone had to go to his home town to have his name written down. So Joseph went with Mary to Bethlehem, the home of King David's family. It was while they were there that Jesus was born. Mary wrapped him in baby-clothes and laid him in a manger, for there was no room for them at the inn. In the fields nearby there were some shepherds minding their sheep. Suddenly they saw a bright light and an angel stood by them. He said to them: "Do not be afraid. I have joyful news for you. Your Saviour is born in David's city. He is Christ, the Lord. You will find him wrapped in baby-clothes, lying in a manger." Then all at once hundreds of angels appeared, praising God: "Glory to God in high heaven; peace on earth to men of good will."

And the shepherds set out at once to find the Saviour.

Christmas

Mass during the day

Prayer

O God, our Father, with joyful hearts we celebrate the birthday of your dear Son, our Saviour Jesus Christ. Give us his love, his joy, his grace, now and for ever.

Lesson

from St Paul's letter to Titus

Dear friend, the goodness and kindness of God, our Saviour, has come to us. He has saved us; not because we have done any good ourselves, but purely out of his own pity and love. He has poured out his Holy Spirit upon us, through Jesus Christ, our Saviour; so that, cleansed from sin by his grace, we may inherit eternal life.

Gospel

according to St Luke

The shepherds said to one another: "Come, let us hurry to Bethlehem and see what has happened; what it is that the Lord has announced to us." They went there, and found Mary and Joseph, and the child lying in the manger. Seeing him, they told what they had heard about this child, and everyone listened to them in amazement. But Mary treasured up these words in her heart. Then the shepherds went home, giving praise and glory to God for everything that they had heard and seen.

Sunday in the Octave of Christmas

Holy Family

Prayer

Lord Jesus Christ, you were always obedient to Mary and Joseph. Make our families holy like yours, so that one day, through the prayers of Mary and Joseph, we may all enjoy the unending family life of heaven; where you live and reign with the Father and the Holy Spirit, one God, for ever and ever.

Lesson

from St Paul's letter to the Colossians

Brothers and sisters, God has chosen you to be his very own; may the peace of Christ reign in your hearts. Be eternally grateful. In everything that you do or say have the thought of the Lord Jesus Christ in your minds.

Gospel

according to St Luke

When Jesus was twelve years old his parents took him to Jerusalem for the feast. When it was all over and everyone set off for home, Jesus stayed behind without his parents knowing. They thought he was with some of their friends. When they realized that he was missing, they went back to look for him, and three days later they found him in the Temple. He was sitting there with the teachers, listening to them and asking them questions. They were all amazed at his intelligence. His mother said to him: "My child, why did you do this to us? Your father and I have been looking for you everywhere. We were terribly worried." And Jesus replied: "Surely you knew that I must be in my Father's house?" He then went back with them to Nazareth and obeyed them in everything. His mother remembered all this as she watched him grow up in mind and body, well-loved by God and man.

Epiphany

January 6

Prayer

On this day, O God, you sent a star to guide the heathen nations to your Son. Our faith is the star that leads us to him in this life. May it bring us one day to heaven, that we may see him in his glory.

Lesson

from the Book of Isaiah, the prophet

Rise up, Jerusalem; shine in the morning light. Your light has come; it is the Lord himself. There is darkness all over the earth, but you are shining in the radiance of God. Those rays of yours will light the heathens on their path; kings will walk in the splendour of your sunrise. People are flocking to you from far-off countries; their caravans are laden with gifts. They are bringing gold and incense, loud in their praises of the Lord.

EPIPHANY

Gospel

according to St Matthew

Soon after Jesus was born, some wise men from the East arrived in Jerusalem, saying: "Where can we find the King of the Jews? A star has proclaimed his birth to us." When King Herod heard this he was greatly disturbed, and so was the whole of Jerusalem. The priests were consulted, and they said that the Prophets had foretold that the King of the Jews would be born in Bethlehem. King Herod, therefore, summoned the wise men and said to them: "Go and look for the child, and then come and tell me where he is, so that I too may worship him." Then the star appeared once more, and it led them to the place where Jesus was. Joyfully they went into the house, and saw Jesus with Mary, his Mother. And they knelt down and worshipped him. Then they opened their store of treasures and gave him gold, incense and myrrh.

They were warned in a dream not to go back to Herod, so they went back to their own country by a different road.

Ash Wednesday

The weeks of the year which come after Epiphany will be found on pp. 114–120

Ash Wednesday

Ashes are blessed in church today.
The priest puts the ashes on our foreheads, saying: 'Remember you are dust, and to dust you will return.'
Lent is a time for doing penance.

Prayer

Lord, give us the strength and courage that we need, so that when we give up things this Lent we will do it with love and generosity.

Lesson

from the Book of Joel, the prophet

What the Lord is saying to you is this: "Come back to me with all your heart. Keep the fast and shed tears for your sins. It is not your garments that I want you to rend, but your hearts." Come back to your Lord and God. He is waiting to forgive you, full of kindness and love. He has no wish to punish you. Take heart and say to him: "Lord, spare your people. Spare us the shame of being mocked at by your enemies because of our wickedness."

Gospel

according to St Matthew

At that time Jesus said to his followers: "When you are fasting do not look solemn and sad, like some people do who want everybody to know that they are fasting. Believe me, they have already had all the reward they are going to get. When you are fasting and doing penance, you must look happy and cheerful, so that no one knows you are fasting, except your Father in heaven. He will know your secret and will reward you."

First Week of Lent

Prayer

O God, during Lent each year you make your Church more holy through her fasting and prayers. Bless these acts of penance that we are doing, and give us all the grace we hope to win by doing them.

Lesson

from St Paul's letter to the Corinthians

Brothers and sisters, I beg you, do not throw away the grace God gives you. This is a holy time, a time of pardon. Never do anything that would get Christians a bad name. Life can be difficult sometimes, but whatever happens always behave as children of God.

FIRST WEEK OF LENT

Gospel

according to St Matthew

At that time the Holy Spirit led Jesus into a desert-place to be tempted by the devil. There he fasted for forty days. When he was very hungry the devil came to him. He showed him the stones that lay there and said to him: "If you are really the Son of God, why not turn those stones into bread?" But Jesus replied: "A man does not live on bread alone; he also lives on every word which God speaks to him." Then the devil took Jesus up to the highest part of the Temple and said to him: "If you are the Son of God, throw yourself down from here, for the Bible says that angels will hold the Lord and prevent him from being hurt on the stones." But Jesus replied: "The Bible also says that it is wrong to put the Lord your God to the test." So the devil finally took Jesus up a high mountain and pointed out to him all the countries of the world and all their splendour. "I will give them all to you," he said, "if you fall down and worship me." But Jesus answered: "Away with you, Satan. It is written in the Bible that you must worship the Lord your God, and serve no one but him." Then the devil left him alone, and angels came to him and waited on him.

Second Week of Lent

Prayer

O God, during Lent each year you make your Church more holy through her fasting and prayers. Bless these acts of penance that we are doing, and give us all the graces we hope to win by doing them.

Lesson

from the First Book of Kings

In those days there was a drought in the land and the Lord said to Elijah: "Go and stay in Zarephath; I have told a widow there to feed you." So Elijah went, and when he came to the gates of the city he saw a widow gathering sticks. He said to her: "Will you get me some water to drink?" As she was going to fetch it, he called after her: "Please bring me a bit of bread also." She replied: "I swear to you by the Lord God that I have nothing to eat, only a handful of meal and a little oil. I am gathering sticks so that I can bake a small cake with it for myself and my son before we die." Elijah said to her: "Don't be afraid, bake a small cake for me first and bring it to me. The Lord God of Israel says to you that you will not run out of meal, nor will you run out of oil, until the Lord sends rain once more upon the earth." The widow did as she was told and the meal and oil lasted out until the drought was ended.

Gospel

according to St Luke

At that time Jesus said to the people: There was a rich man who was clothed in purple and fine linen and who feasted every day. And at the gate lay a poor man named Lazarus, full of sores. He begged to be fed with what fell from the rich man's table, but only the dogs came and licked his sores.

The poor man died, and angels carried him to Abraham's side.

The rich man also died, and was buried in Hell. Lifting up his eyes he saw Abraham, far off, and Lazarus at his side. And he called out: "Father Abraham, take pity on me and send Lazarus to dip the end of his fingers in water and cool my tongue, for I am tormented by fire." But Abraham said: "Son, remember that you received your good things in your lifetime, while Lazarus had nothing but evil things. There is a great chasm between us now. Lazarus could not come to you, even if he wanted to." "Then

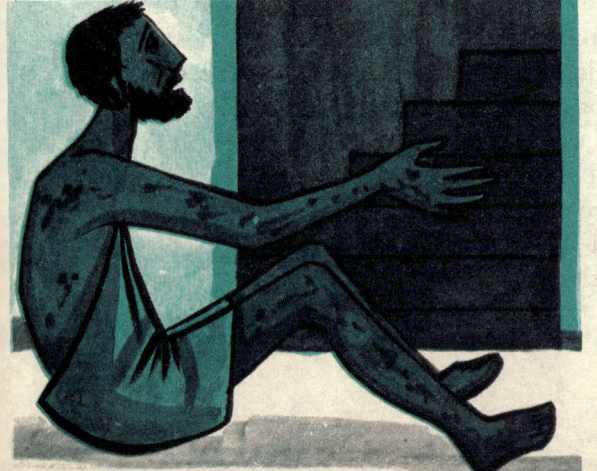

send him to my father's house for I have five brothers. Let him warn them, so that they may not also come to this place of torment." Abraham said:

"But they have Moses and the prophets." "I know," he said, "but if someone comes to them from the dead, they will listen and do penance." "If they do not listen to Moses and the prophets," said Abraham, "they will not be convinced even if someone comes back from the dead."

Third Week of Lent

Prayer

Father forgive us when we do wrong and help us to forgive other people when they do wrong to us.

Lesson

from the Second Book of Kings

In those days the wife of one of the sons of the prophets cried to Elisha: "My husband has died owing money, and now the creditor has come to take away my two children to be his slaves." Elisha said to her: "What do you want me to do? Tell me, what have you got in your house?" And she said: "I have nothing except a jar of oil." Then he said to her: "Go and borrow as many empty jars as you can from your neighbours. Then go indoors and fill them from the jar of oil which you have." She did so, and as she filled the jars there was always more oil left over, until the last jar was full. Then Elisha said: "Go, sell the oil and pay your debts, and you and your sons can live on the oil that remains."

FOURTH WEEK OF LENT

Gospel

according to St Matthew

At that time Jesus said to his disciples: "Truly, I say to you, whatever you bind on earth will be bound in heaven, and whatever you loose on earth will be loosed in heaven. Again I say to you if two of you agree on earth about anything you ask, my Father in heaven will give it to you. For where two or three are gathered together in my name, there am I in the midst of them."

Then Peter came to him and said; "Lord, how often shall my brother sin against me, and I forgive him? As many as seven times?" Jesus said to him: "No not seven times, but seventy times seven times."

Fourth Week of Lent

Prayer

Forgive us, Father, all the wrong we have done, and give us new life through our Lord Jesus Christ, your Son.

Lesson

from the Second Book of Kings

In those days a widow woman came to the prophet Elisha on Mount Carmel and said to him: "Did I not ask my Lord for a son? And now he is dead." Then Elisha said to his servant Gehazi: "Go to the widow's house, and lay my staff upon the face of the child."

FOURTH WEEK OF LENT

Gehazi did so, but there was no sound or sign of life. So he went back to Elisha and said: "The child has not awakened." Elisha went to the house and saw the child lying dead on his bed. So he shut the door upon the two of them, and prayed to the Lord. Then he lay upon the child, putting his mouth upon the child's mouth, his eyes upon his eyes, and his hands upon his hands, and as he stretched himself upon him, the child's flesh became warm. At last the child sneezed seven times, and opened his eyes. Then Elisha called Gehazi and said to him: "Fetch the widow woman." She came and fell at his feet bowing to the ground. Then she took her son and went out.

Gospel
according to St Luke

At that time Jesus went to a city called Naim, and his disciples and a great crowd went with him. As he came to the gate of the city, a dead man was being carried out, the only son of his mother who was a widow. A large crowd of people from the city was with her. When Jesus saw her, he was sorry for her and said to her "Do not weep." Then he said to the dead man: "Young man, I say to you arise", and the dead man sat up and began to speak. Everyone was amazed, and praised God, saying: "A great prophet has come among us. God has visited his people."

The Fifth Week of Lent

Prayer

O God, our Father, help us at this time to think about the sufferings of your dear Son, Jesus Christ. Make us love him so much that no kind of temptation will ever be able to separate us from him.

Lesson

from the Book of Daniel

In those days the Babylonians said to their King: "Hand Daniel over to us, or else we will kill you and your household." The King saw that there was no way out, and he handed Daniel over to them. They threw Daniel into a den of lions, and he was there for six days, but the lions did not touch him.

Now the prophet Habakkuk was in Judea. He had boiled pottage and had broken bread into a bowl, and was going into a field to take it to the reapers. But the angel of the Lord said to Habakkuk: "Take the dinner which you have to Babylon, to Daniel, in the lions' den." And he lifted him up by the hair of his head and sat him down in Babylon right over the den. So Daniel was given food.

On the seventh day the King came to mourn for Daniel. When he came to the den he looked in, and there sat Daniel. And the King cried out: "You are great, Lord God of Daniel, and there is no other

God besides you." And he pulled Daniel out, and threw into the den the men who had tried to kill Daniel. And at once the lions came and ate them up.

Gospel

according to St John

At that time the chief priests and the Pharisees met together and said: "What are we to do? for this man Jesus is working many miracles, and if we let him go on like this everyone will believe in him, and the Romans will come and destroy our temple and our nation." Then Caiaphas, the high priest of the year, said to them: "Don't you realize that it is necessary for one man to die for the people, otherwise the whole nation will perish." So from that day on they made plans to put Jesus to death. Jesus, therefore, no longer went about openly among the Jews. He went to the country near the desert, to a town called Ephraim, and stayed there with his disciples.

Passion Sunday (Palm Sunday)

The Blessing of Palms

Prayer
O God, bless these palms which we will carry to remind us that we are loyal soldiers of your Son, Jesus Christ our Lord.

Gospel

according to St Matthew

Jesus was on his way to Jerusalem. When he came to a village not far from the city, he said to two of his disciples: "Go into the village and you will find there a she-ass with a foal at her side. Bring them to me." The disciples did as they were told. They spread their cloaks on the ass and helped Jesus to mount. The people came flocking from the city to meet Jesus. They spread out their garments in his path and strewed the way with branches cut down from the trees. They crowded round him, shouting "Hosanna for the Son of David. Blessed is he who comes in the name of the Lord!"

The Mass

Prayer

Almighty God, our Saviour became a man like us and died for us on the cross. What a wonderful example of humility! Help us to follow his example, to be patient like he was, and so to share in that new life to which he rose again from the grave. We ask you this through Jesus Christ, your Son, our Lord.

HOLY THURSDAY

Lesson

from St Paul's letter to the Philippians

Brothers and sisters, you must be like Jesus Christ. Even though he was God he did not cling to the magnificence that was his due as God. He laid it all aside and became man, just like every other man. He became humble and obedient to the point of accepting death—even death on a cross. That is why God has raised him to such a height and given him a name that is greater than any other name. At the name of Jesus every one in heaven and on earth must kneel; everyone must proclaim that the Lord Jesus Christ dwells in the glory of God the Father.

The Passion

See "A Play for Good Friday", p. 88

Holy Thursday

The Mass is in the evening, for it was then that our Lord ate the Last Supper with his apostles.

Prayer

God our Father, we are here to share in the meal which Jesus gave us before he died, to show us how much he loves us. Make us always love him in return and everyone else for his sake. He lives and reigns with you and the Holy Spirit, one God, for ever and ever.

Lesson

from St Paul's letter to the Corinthians

Brothers and sisters, on the night our Lord Jesus was betrayed, he took some bread in his hands, and when he had given thanks, he broke it and said: "Take this and eat it. This is my body, which I have offered up for you. Do this in memory of me." When supper was finished, he took the chalice and said: "This chalice is the new testament in my blood. Whenever you drink it, do this in memory of me."

And so whenever you eat this bread and drink from this chalice, you are announcing the Lord's death until he comes again. If anyone, therefore, eats this bread or drinks from the Lord's chalice unworthily, he will be guilty of the Lord's death.

Gospel

according to St John

Jesus knew that the time had come for him to die. Judas had already left. He was on his way to betray his master. But Jesus wanted to give his apostles one further proof of his love for them. So he got up from the table, laid his garments aside, took a towel and girded himself with it. Then he poured some water in a basin and began to wash his disciples' feet. Peter

HOLY THURSDAY

said: "You are never going to wash my feet!" But Jesus answered: "If I do not wash you, it means that you will not be with me in the kingdom of heaven."

Then Peter said to him: "If that is so, then wash not only my feet, but my hands and my head too." Jesus replied: "A man who has bathed does not need to do more than wash the stains from his feet, and he is clean all over." But Jesus knew he had been betrayed, so he added: "Not all of you are clean." Then Jesus put on his garments again and said: "What I have done is what you must do to each other. You must follow my example."

The Washing of the Feet

In many churches the priest now washes the feet of twelve men or boys, like Jesus did.

Hymn
Where is love and loving kindness

Prayer
Have mercy on us, Lord. You washed your disciples' feet, and we have followed your example. Wash away all our sins, for you are God, living and reigning for ever and ever.

After Mass the Blessed Sacrament is taken to a special altar called the "altar of repose". We go there to worship our Lord before we leave the church. The cloths are then taken off the High Altar. It is left quite bare.

A play for Good Friday

Scene 1

Gethsemane

Jesus and the eleven disciples

JESUS: Sit down here while I go and pray. But you, Peter, James and John, come with me. Do not go to sleep; stay awake and keep me company.

He goes a short distance from them, and kneels down in prayer.

My Father, if it is possible, take this chalice of suffering away from me; but your will must be done, not mine.

After a little while he goes back to his disciples and finds them asleep. He rouses Peter.

Peter, could you not stay awake and keep me company for just an hour? Keep awake and say your prayers, so as not to give way to temptation.

He goes back and prays.

A PLAY FOR GOOD FRIDAY

Father, if this chalice cannot pass from me, I shall drink it, for your will must be done.

He goes back to the disciples and wakes them up.

Get up now; we must be on our way. The person who is going to betray me is near at hand.

Enter Judas with a band of soldiers. He goes up to Jesus and kisses him.

JUDAS: Hail, Master.
JESUS: My friend, why have you come? To betray me with a kiss?

The soldiers come and take Jesus prisoner. Peter rushes up, waving his sword.

PETER: Leave it to me, Master. I will save you.
JESUS: Peter, put your sword away. If I needed any help I could ask my Father, and he would send armies of angels to defend me. But everything must happen that was foretold by the prophets about me.

He turns to the soldiers.

You have come with swords and clubs to arrest me as though I were a robber, and yet I used to sit teaching close to you, day after day, and you never laid hands on me. But this is your hour, the hour of darkness. Come, lead me away.

Scene 2

Jesus before Caiaphas

Jesus, Caiaphas and priests, three accusers, servants. Peter at side stage, warming himself at a fire.

FIRST ACCUSER: I distinctly heard this man say that we must not pay taxes to Caesar.

CAIAPHAS: And what has the prisoner to say to that?

Jesus is silent.

SECOND ACCUSER: He has been going all over the country stirring up the people to rebellion. He has broken all the laws of our religion and even works on the Sabbath day, defying the priests. He claims to be the Christ, the Son of God.

CAIAPHAS: Has the prisoner nothing to say to all these accusations?

Jesus is again silent.

SERVANT: *(in a loud whisper to Peter)* You were with Jesus the Galilean.

PETER: I have no idea what you are talking about.

SECOND SERVANT: You are certainly one of them; your very speech gives you away.

PETER: I tell you, I know nothing about this man.

Peter leaves hurriedly.

THIRD ACCUSER: I was there when this man threw people out of the Temple. He threatened to destroy it and said he could build it up again in three days.
CAIAPHAS: Once again I ask you, what have you to say for yourself? . . . In the name of the living God I command you to tell us if you are the Christ, the Son of God.
JESUS: It is as you say; and one day you will see me, the Son of Man, sitting at God's right hand and coming on the clouds of heaven.
CAIAPHAS: You heard him? He has the wickedness to call upon God to back his lies. What is your verdict?
ALL: He must be put to death; he must be put to death.

Scene 3

Jesus before Pilate

Jesus, Caiaphas and priests, Pilate, soldiers.
PILATE: What charge do you bring against this man?
CAIAPHAS: He is a criminal, of course, otherwise we would not have brought him to you.
PILATE: Why don't you take him and judge him according to your law?
CAIAPHAS: We have no power to put anyone to death.
PILATE: What has he done that is worthy of death?
CAIAPHAS: He has gone about stirring up the people and claiming to be a king.
PILATE: *(To Jesus)* Are you a king? Are you the king of the Jews?

JESUS: Is this what you yourself think, or is it just what others have told you?
PILATE: Am I a Jew? It is your own nation and its chief priests who have given you up to me. What is your crime?
JESUS: My kingdom is not an earthly kingdom. If it were, my servants would be fighting for me. They would not let me fall into the hands of the Jews.
PILATE: You are a king, then?
JESUS: It is as you say. I am a king. I came into the world to proclaim the truth. If you love the truth, you will listen to my words.
PILATE: What is truth?

(to the Jews) I can find nothing wrong with this man. I will have him scourged and that will be the end of it.

Jesus is led away.

CAIAPHAS If you release this man you are no friend of Caesar.
PILATE: I tell you, I can find nothing wrong with him. But this is what I will do. You have a custom of demanding that I should release one prisoner at Paschal time. Very well, then. Shall I release this man, the king of the Jews, or shall I release Barabbas?
ALL: Barabbas, not this man.
PILATE: But Barabbas is a robber and a murderer.
ALL: We want Barabbas; we want Barabbas.
PILATE: Then what shall I do with Jesus?
ALL: Crucify him.

Jesus is led on to the stage with a crown of thorns and a scarlet cloak.

PILATE: Just look at this man!
ALL: Crucify him, crucify him!
PILATE: Shall I crucify your king?
ALL: We have no king but Caesar.
PILATE: Fetch me some water.

Two servants enter with basin and towel. Pilate washes his hands.

I wash my hands of the blood of this innocent man. You do what you like.
ALL: His blood be upon us and upon our children.

Scene 4
Jesus on the Cross

Jesus, Mary, John, Caiaphas and priests, soldiers.
CAIAPHAS: Now save yourself, you who said that you could rebuild the Temple in three days. Come down from that cross and we will believe you.
PRIESTS: He saved others, but he cannot save himself.

Enter Pilate with an inscription.

PILATE: Here, I have an inscription for you to put on his cross.
CAIAPHAS: What does it say?
PILATE: It is written in three languages, Hebrew, Greek and Latin, and it says: "Jesus of Nazareth, the king of the Jews."
CAIAPHAS: That's wrong. You mustn't say "the king of the Jews" but, "He said: 'I am the king of the Jews'".

A PLAY FOR GOOD FRIDAY

PILATE: What I have written, I have written.

He hangs the inscription on the cross and goes out.

JESUS: Father, forgive them; they know not what they do.
MARY: Father, forgive them.
JESUS: Mother, behold your son. *(To John)* Son, behold your mother.

John goes to Mary and supports her on his arm.

JESUS: I am thirsty.

A soldier puts a reed on a sponge and holds it to Jesus' mouth.

JESUS: Into your hands, O Lord, I commend my spirit.

He drinks the vinegar and cries out:

It is achieved!

He hangs his head and dies.
Darkness and thunder. After a pause, the lights come up.

CENTURION: Truly, this was the Son of God.
ALL: *(kneeling)* Truly, this was the Son of God, and we believed that he was a sinner, rejected by God. But God will raise him up and exalt him, and give him a name above every other name.
Jesus, my Lord and my God.

A hymn is sung.

Holy Communion on Good Friday

All say the "Our Father".
The priest holds up a host and says:

P. This is the Lamb of God
    who takes away the sins of the world.
    Happy are those who are called to his supper.
All Lord, I am not worthy to receive you;
    but only say the word and I shall be healed.

Prayer after Communion

Almighty and merciful God, you have brought home to us the suffering and death of your Son, Jesus Christ. Have mercy on us; forgive us our sins; strengthen our faith; and give us everlasting life. We ask you this through Jesus Christ our Lord.

Easter Vigil
Holy Saturday

These short services can, if desired, be conducted in the classroom after the Easter holidays.

1. The Paschal Candle

NOTE: The parish priest will probably have an old paschal candle which he can give to the school. Alternatively, the class can obtain their own candle and suitably decorate it.

A child is given the paschal candle to hold in front of the class. Another child lights it with a taper.
A third child reads the following prayer:

O God, in sending us your Son, Jesus Christ, you have made your light shine forth in the darkness of this world, and you have warmed our hearts with his love. Make us pure and holy, so that one day we may see in heaven your light that never fails. We ask you this through Jesus Christ our Lord.
All **Amen.**

The child holds the candle up high and says:

The Light of Christ.

All genuflect and say:

O God, we thank you.

All sit down. The reader goes to the front and reads:

A reading from the Book of Genesis.
In the beginning God created the heavens and the earth. The earth was bare and empty, and darkness covered the waters. But the Spirit of God was stirring over the waters, and God said: "Let there be light",

and there was light. God saw the light was good. He separated the light from the darkness, calling the light Day and the darkness Night. And there was an evening and morning, the first day.

Let us pray:

O God, how wonderfully you created the world, and yet how more wonderfully you redeemed it. Keep us from falling into sin, for we want to be happy with you and enjoy your light for ever and ever in heaven, through Christ our Lord.

All **Amen.**

A hymn is sung, expressing joy in the light of Christ.

2. Baptismal water

A child holds a glass dish and another child pours holy water into it from a jug. A third child reads the following prayer:

Almighty, ever-living God, you have given us this holy water to remind us of the water of our baptism, when new life was given to us and we became your loving children. Show us now the power of your love and send us your Holy Spirit, through Jesus Christ our Lord.

All **Amen.**

The children come forward one by one, take holy water and cross themselves.
Then the reader goes to the front and reads:

EASTER VIGIL

A reading from the Book of the Exodus.
At that time the Egyptians chased the Israelites and came up with them where they were camping by the sea. Then Moses stretched out his hand over the sea and the waters parted. The sons of Israel went on dry ground right into the sea, with walls of water to right and left of them. The Egyptians gave chase: after them they went, right into the sea, all Pharaoh's house, his chariots and his horsemen. When the sons of Israel had reached the other side, the Lord said to Moses: "Stretch out your hand over the sea, that the waters may flow back on the Egyptians and their chariots and their horsemen." Moses did so, and as day broke, the sea returned to its bed and drowned the chariots and the horsemen of Pharaoh's whole army; not a single one of them was left. But the sons of Israel had marched through the sea on dry ground, walls of water to right and left of them.
Let us pray:
O God, we have seen how you once saved your chosen people by your wonderful power. Today you are the Saviour of all peoples. Let everyone know you and love you through Jesus Christ our Lord.
All **Amen.** *A hymn is sung, expressing Easter joy.*

Easter Sunday

Prayer

Today, O God, through your Son's conquest of death, you opened for us the door to eternal life. You have made us long for heaven; help us to get there.

Epistle
from St Paul's letter to the Corinthians

Brothers and sisters, you must be pure, like new bread. Our Saviour has been offered in sacrifice for us, and we must now live pure and holy lives, free from wickedness and sin.

Gospel

according to St Mark

Some of the women bought spices with which to anoint the body of Jesus. They came to the tomb very early in the morning, and said to each other: "Whom shall we find to roll back the stone from the door of the tomb?" Then they looked and saw that the stone, great as it was, had already been rolled away. They went into the tomb and saw there a young man dressed in white. The young man said to them: "Do not be afraid. You have come looking for Jesus of Nazareth who was crucified; he has risen again; he is not here. Here is the place where they laid him. Go and tell Peter and the rest of his disciples that he is going before you into Galilee. There you shall see him, as he promised you."

Second Week of Easter

Prayer

Holy Lord and Father, you sent your Son Jesus Christ to be our good shepherd who laid down his life for his sheep. Help us to follow him wherever he leads us.

Lesson

from the Acts of the Apostles

In those days an angel of the Lord said to the apostle Philip: "Go southwards along the road from Jerusalem to Gaza." Philip did so and he came upon an Ethiopian, sitting in his chariot and reading the book of the prophet Isaiah. Philip said to him: "Do you understand what you are reading?" "How can I," he said, "unless someone helps me?" And he invited Philip to come up and sit with him. Now the passage of the Bible he was reading was this: "He was led like a sheep to the slaughter, and like a lamb before his shearer he opened not his mouth."

The Ethiopian said to Philip: "Whom is he talking about, himself or someone else?" Then Philip, beginning with this passage of the Bible told him the good news of Jesus. As they went along the road they came to some water, and the Ethiopian said: "Look,

SECOND WEEK OF EASTER

there is water; why cannot I be baptized?" And they both got down from the chariot and went into the water, and Philip baptized him.

Gospel

according to St John

At that time Mary Magdalene was standing weeping outside the tomb of Jesus, and looking into the tomb she saw two angels dressed in white. "Why are you weeping?" they said to her, and Mary answered: "Because they have taken away my Lord, and I do not know where they have laid him." She turned as she spoke, and she saw Jesus standing near her, but she did not know that it was Jesus. She thought he was the gardener, and she said to him: "Sir, if you have taken him away, tell me where you have laid him." Jesus said to her: "Mary". She turned and said to him "Rabboni", which means "my master." Jesus said to her: "Do not touch me; I have not yet ascended to the Father. But go and tell my disciples, I am ascending to my Father and your father, to my God and your God."

Third Week of Easter

Prayer

O God, it is your will that all men should come to know the truth and be saved. Send out apostles, then, to tell the good news to all mankind, so that all may come to know you and your Son, Jesus Christ our Lord.

Lesson
from the Acts of the Apostles

At that time Peter said to the Jews: "This is the good news which is proclaimed throughout all Judea: God has anointed Jesus of Nazareth with the Holy Spirit and with power. He went about doing good and healing all who were possessed by the devil; for God was with him. And we saw all that he did in the country of the Jews and in Jerusalem. They put him to death on a cross, but God raised him on the third day. He appeared, not to everybody, but to us who were chosen by God to be his witnesses, and we ate and drank with him after he rose from the dead. And he commanded us to preach to the people and to tell them that everyone who believes in him will receive forgiveness."

Gospel
according to St Matthew

At that time the eleven disciples went to Galilee, to the mountain where Jesus had told them to go. And when they saw Jesus there they worshipped him, but some of them doubted. Then Jesus said to them: "All power in heaven and earth has been given to me. Go therefore, into the whole world, and make all men my disciples, baptizing them in the name of the Father and of the Son, and of the Holy Spirit. Teach them to do all that I have told you. I will be with you always to the end of the world."

Fourth Week of Easter

Prayer

Holy Lord and Father, by the death and resurrection of your Son Jesus Christ you have called us out of darkness into your marvellous light. Make us a holy people, so that we may always love you and do your will.

Epistle

from the first letter of St Peter

Dear brothers and sisters, put away all malice and deceit and insincerity and envy and slander. You are a chosen race, a royal priesthood, a holy nation, God's own people. You have been chosen to tell the world about the wonderful things that God has done. He called you out of darkness into his marvellous light. Once you were no people at all; now you are God's people. Once you had received no mercy; now you have received mercy.

Gospel

according to St John

At that time Simon Peter was fishing with some of the disciples and Jesus appeared to them on the shore. When they got out on land, they saw a charcoal fire there, with fish lying on it, and bread. Jesus said to them: "Bring some of the fish that you have caught, and come and have breakfast."

When they had finished breakfast, Jesus said to Simon Peter: "Simon son of John, do you love me more than these?" Peter said to him: "Yes, Lord, you know that I love you." Jesus said: "Feed my lambs." A second time he said to him: "Simon son of John, do you love me?" Peter said to him: "Lord, you know that I love you." Jesus said: "Tend my sheep." Jesus said to him a third time: "Simon, son of John, do you love me?" Peter was grieved because he said this a third time. And he said to him: "Lord, you know everything; you know that I love you." Jesus said to him: "Feed my sheep."

Fifth Week of Easter

Prayer

O God, there is no end to your kindness, no limit to your gifts. We thank you for all your gifts and especially for hearing our prayers through Jesus Christ, our Lord.

Epistle
from the letter of St James, Apostle

Dear brothers and sisters, confess your sins to one another and pray for one another, that you may be healed. The prayers of a good person are very powerful. Elijah was a man as we are, and when he prayed that it might not rain, no rain fell on the earth for three years and six months. Then he prayed for rain, and the rain came and the earth was fruitful.

Gospel
according to St Luke

At that time Jesus said to the people: "If a friend of yours comes to you at midnight and asks you to lend him three loaves you will say: 'Don't bother me. The door is bolted and we are all in bed. I cannot get up and give you anything.' But if your friend keeps on asking you, in the end you will get up and give him what he wants. Ask, and you will receive; seek, and

ASCENSION

you will find; knock, and the door will be opened to you. What father among you, if his son asks for a fish, will give him a snake instead; or, if his son asks for an egg, will give him a scorpion? You know how to give your children good things; how much more will the heavenly Father give the Holy Spirit to those who ask him!"

Ascension

Prayer

Almighty God, we believe that on this day Jesus, our Redeemer, went up into heaven. Let us often think of heaven and long for it.

Lesson

from the Acts of the Apostles

Jesus gave his apostles many proofs that he was still alive. For forty days after his sufferings he appeared to them several times and told them about the kingdom of God. One day, when he was sitting at table with them, he told them not to leave Jerusalem but to wait there until he sent them the Holy Spirit. The words he said were these: "John baptized you with water, but very soon now you will be baptized with the Holy Spirit." The apostles asked him when he was going to restore the kingdom of Israel. Jesus replied that it was not for man to know what God's plans were. "When you have received the Holy Spirit," he said, "you will be strong, and you will

preach in Jerusalem, throughout Judea, and all over the world."

When he had said this, the apostles saw Jesus lifted up into heaven, and a cloud hid him from their sight. They were still looking up towards heaven when two men appeared at their side, dressed in white. "Men of Galilee," they said, "why do you stand there looking up to heaven? Jesus will come back in the same way as you have seen him going up into heaven."

Gospel

according to St Mark

One day Jesus appeared to the eleven disciples as they sat at table. He blamed them for their lack of faith, and then said to them: "Go out into the whole world and preach the good news to everyone. He who believes and is baptized will be saved. Where believers go, these signs will go with them: they will cast out devils in my name, they will speak in tongues that are strange to them; they will take up serpents in their hands, and drink poison without harm; they will lay their hands upon the sick and make them well again." When Jesus had finished speaking to them, he was taken up into heaven, and sits now at the right hand of God. And the disciples went out and preached everywhere. God was with them, and worked miracles to prove the truth of what they said.

Pentecost

Ten days after the Ascension, fifty days after Easter, the Holy Spirit came down on the disciples gathered together in the upper room in Jerusalem. This is the great event we are celebrating today. Let us ask the Holy Spirit to dwell in the hearts of all Christians.

Prayer

O God, on this day you filled the disciples with the strength and love of the Holy Spirit. Fill us too with the Holy Spirit, that we may have wisdom, strength and joy.

Lesson

from the Acts of the Apostles

On the day of Pentecost the disciples were gathered together in the upper room. Suddenly a sound came from heaven like that of a strong wind blowing. It filled the whole house where they were sitting. Then there appeared to them what seemed to be tongues of fire which parted and came to rest on each of them. Then they were filled with the Holy Spirit, and began to speak in strange languages. There were people at that time in Jerusalem from every part of the world. When they heard what had happened they came together in crowds, and were amazed to hear the disciples speaking to them about Jesus, each in his own language. "Are they not all Galileans speaking?" they asked. "How is it that each of us hears them talking about God's wonders, each in his own native tongue?"

Gospel

according to St John

Jesus said to his disciples: "If a man has any love for me, he will be true to my word, and my Father will love him. We will come to him and dwell with him. The man who has no love for me is not true to my word. And this word, which you have been hearing from me, comes not from me, but from my Father who sent me. The Holy Spirit, whom the Father will send in my name, will teach you everything, and remind you of everything that I have told you. Peace is the gift that I leave with you, the peace that is mine to give. Do not let your heart be distressed. I am going to the Father, but I will come back to you again.

"Satan, the ruler of this world, stands waiting, but he has no power over me. But the world must be convinced that I love the Father, and act only as the Father has commanded me to act."

Trinity Sunday

Prayer

Almighty God, you have made known to us the glorious mystery of your Trinity—one God, three persons. We believe and worship. Strengthen our faith, and keep us safe from everything that can harm us.

Epistle

from St Paul's letter to the Romans

How deep is the mine of God's wisdom, of his knowledge; we can never hope to understand all that he does! Who has ever understood the Lord's thoughts, or given him advice? He made everything; and nothing can exist without him. To him be glory for ever and ever. Amen.

Gospel

according to St Matthew

Jesus said to his disciples: "All power in heaven and earth has been given to me. You, therefore, must go out and make disciples of all nations, and baptize them in the name of the Father, and of the Son, and of the Holy Ghost. You must teach them to keep all the commandments I have given to you. Behold, I am with you all through the days that are coming, until the end of the world."

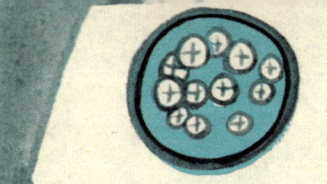

The Body and Blood of the Lord
Corpus Christi
Prayer

O God, we offer you this Mass to thank you for the wonderful gift of the body and blood of your Son, Jesus Christ, who died for us on the cross. Give us Jesus in communion, so that we may all live together in close union with him.

Epistle
from St Paul's letter to the Corinthians

Brothers and sisters, this is what the Lord told me, and what I now pass on to you:

On the night on which he was betrayed, the Lord Jesus took bread in his hands, and when he had given thanks, he broke it and said: "Take this and eat it. This is my body, which I have offered up for you. Do this in memory of me."

When supper was finished, he took the chalice and said: "Take this chalice. It is the new testament in my blood. Whenever you drink it, do this in memory of me." And so whenever you eat this bread and drink from this chalice, you are announcing the Lord's death until he comes again. If anyone, therefore eats this bread or drinks from the Lord's chalice unworthily, he will be guilty of the Lord's body and blood. We must therefore examine ourselves carefully before we go to communion.

SACRED HEART

Gospel

according to St John

At that time Jesus said to the Jews: "My flesh is real food, my blood is real drink. He who eats my flesh and drinks my blood, lives continually in me and I in him. As I live because of the Father, the living Father who has sent me, so he who eats me will live, in his turn, because of me.

"Such is the bread that has come down from heaven; it is not like the manna which your fathers ate in the desert, and died none the less. The man who eats this bread will live forever."

The Sacred Heart

Prayer

By our sins, O God, we have wounded the heart of your Son; even so you love us; even so you have mercy on us. Help us to love Jesus with all our hearts, and to serve him with joy.

Epistle

from St Paul's letter to the Ephesians

Brothers and sisters, I am the least of all the saints, yet God has given me the privilege of preaching the good news of salvation to the pagan nations, of telling them about the wonderful riches of Christ's kingdom. There were God's secrets. They have been kept hidden since the very beginning of the world; but now everyone is to know them. The Church must tell the world what God planned in his wisdom, what he has done through Jesus Christ, our Lord. May Christ live in your hearts, that you may know how great is Christ's love for you.

Gospel
according to St John

The Jews would not let the bodies remain crucified on the sabbath, because that sabbath day was a solemn one. They therefore asked Pilate to order someone to break their legs and take them away. The soldiers broke the legs of the two thieves who were crucified with Jesus, but when they came to Jesus they found that he was already dead. So they did not break his legs, but one of the soldiers pierced his side with a spear, and blood and water came flowing out.

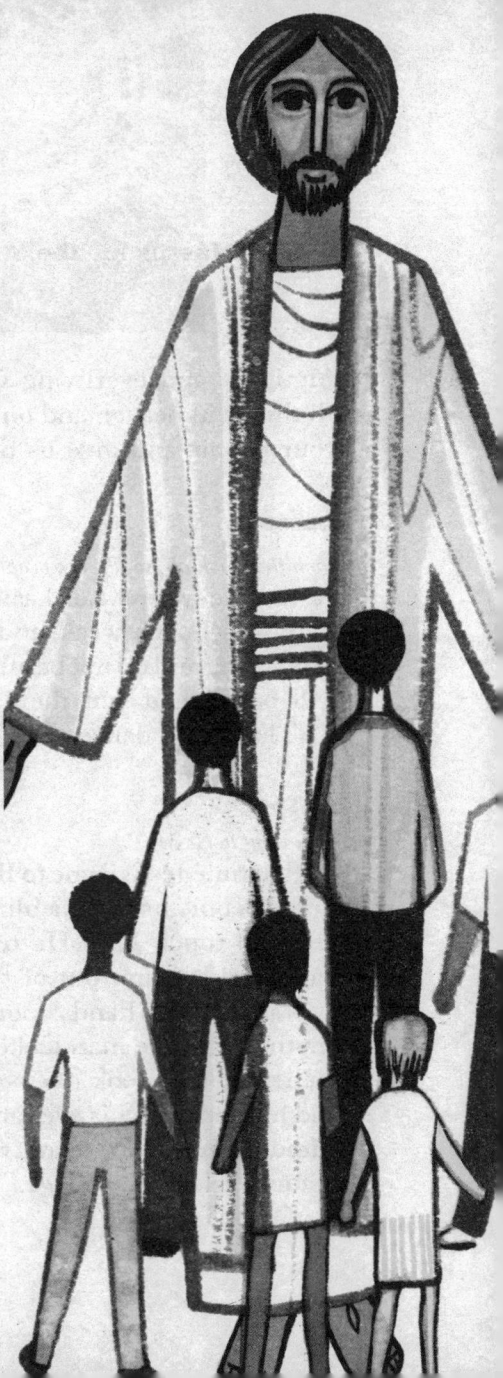

Six Masses for the Weeks after Epiphany
I

Prayer

Almighty and everliving God, you are the ruler of all things in heaven and on earth. Hear the prayers of your people and give us peace.

Lesson

from the Book of Isaiah, the prophet

In those days the Lord said to Isaiah: Give strength to those who are weak, and say to those who are sad: "Be strong and do not be afraid." The eyes of the blind will be opened and the ears of the deaf will hear. The lame will dance and the dumb will sing for joy.

Gospel

according to St Mark

At that time Jesus came to Bethsaida with his disciples. Some people brought a blind man to him and begged Jesus to touch him. He took the blind man by the hand and led him out of the village. He spat on his eyes and laid his hands upon him, saying: "Do you see anything?" The man looked up and said: "I can see men; but they look like walking trees." Again Jesus laid his hands on his eyes and the man was completely cured. Jesus sent him away to his home, saying: "Do not go back to the village."

WEEKS AFTER EPIPHANY
II

Prayer

Almighty and everliving God, without you we are weak and can do nothing. Look on us with love, and protect us with your strong right hand.

Epistle
from St Paul's letter to the Hebrews

Dear brothers and sisters; without faith it is impossible to please God. If you wish to be near God you must believe that he really exists and that he rewards those who seek him. Noah had faith; that is why he left his house in search of a new land, and so became the father of a great nation.

Gospel
according to St Luke

At that time, when Jesus had come down from the mountain with Peter, James and John, a great crowd met him, and a man from the crowd cried out: "Teacher, look upon my son. He is my only child, but an evil spirit has taken hold of him and he rolls on the ground and foams at the mouth and the spirit will not leave him. I asked your disciples to rid him of this spirit, but they could not do it." Then Jesus said: "Bring your son here." He spoke sharply to the wicked spirit, cured the boy, and gave him back to his father. And everyone was amazed at the power of God.

WEEKS AFTER EPIPHANY

III

Prayer

Almighty and everliving God, without you we are weak and can do nothing. Look on us with love, and protect us with your strong right hand.

Epistle

from St John's letter to the churches

Dear brothers and sisters: if we keep the commandments of God and do what he wants, Christ will give us anything we ask. Now this is God's commandment: that we believe in the name of his Son Jesus Christ and love one another. If we do this, he will live in us and we will live in him. And we will know for sure that he is living in us, because he will give us the Holy Spirit.

Gospel

according to St John

At that time, when it was evening, the disciples went down to the sea, got into a boat, and started off across the sea to Capernaum. Jesus was not with them. It grew dark and a strong wind got up. When they had rowed about three or four miles, they saw Jesus walking on the sea towards them. They were very frightened, but Jesus said: "It is I; do not be afraid". They were glad to have him with them in the boat, and they soon came to land.

WEEKS AFTER EPIPHANY

IV

Prayer

Almighty and everliving God, without you we are weak and can do nothing. Look on us with love, and protect us with your strong right hand.

Epistle

from St Paul's letter to the Thessalonians

Dear brothers and sisters: we are always thanking God for you and remembering you in our prayers. We tell God our Father how strong your faith is, how much you love him and show your love in everything you do, and how much you hope in our Lord Jesus Christ.

Everyone is learning how you welcomed us and how you gave up your idols and turned to the living and true God. And now you are waiting for his Son Jesus to come again from heaven: Jesus, whom God raised from the dead and who saves us from the just anger of God.

Gospel

according to St John

At that time Jesus was on his way once again to Cana in Galilee, where he had changed water into wine. At Capernaum there was an official whose son was ill.

When he heard that Jesus was there, he went and begged him to come to heal his son who was dying. Jesus said to him: "Unless you see signs and wonders you will not believe." The official said to him: "Sir, come before my child dies." Jesus said to him: "Go: your son will live." The man believed what Jesus said to him and went home. His son was well again.

V

Prayer

Almighty and everliving God, with you we are weak and can do nothing. Look on us with love, and protect us with your strong right hand.

Epistle

from the letter of St James, Apostle

Dear brothers and sisters: If you are in pain, pray to God. If you are happy, sing God's praises. If one of you is sick, send for the priests. They will pray over the sick man and anoint him with oil in the name of the Lord. Their prayer of faith will save the sick man and the Lord will raise him up. If he has sinned, God will forgive him. Tell one another your sins and pray for one another that you may be healed. The prayer of a good man is very powerful.

Gospel

according to St Matthew

At that time Jesus was in the district of Tyre and Sidon, and a Canaanite woman came to him and cried: "Have mercy on me, O Lord, Son of David; my daughter is possessed by a devil." Jesus did not answer her and his disciples said to him: "Send her away, she is pestering us with her cries." Jesus said to her: "I was sent only to the lost sheep of the house of Israel." But she came and knelt before him and said: "Lord help me." He answered: "It is not fair to take the children's bread and throw it to the dogs." But she said: "Yes, Lord, yet even the dogs eat the crumbs that fall from their master's table." Then Jesus said to her: "O woman, great is your faith. You may have what you asked." And her daughter was healed instantly.

VI

Prayer

Father, almighty and everliving God, make us always truly wise. Help us to understand what you want us to do, and give us the strength to do it. We ask you this through Jesus Christ your Son, our Lord.

WEEKS AFTER EPIPHANY

Lesson

from the First Book of Kings

In those days the Lord said to Solomon in a dream: "Ask me for anything you like." And Solomon said: "Lord, you always showed such great love towards my father, king David. And now you have made me king, even though I am little more than a child. I do not know how to rule. Give me wisdom, so that I shall be able to tell right from wrong and rule your people well."

The Lord was pleased with Solomon for asking this, and said to him: "Because you asked for wisdom and not for long life and riches and power over your enemies, I will make you so wise that you will be the wisest man that ever lived. No one will ever be wiser than you.

Gospel

according to St Matthew

At that time Jesus said to his people: "Whoever hears my words and does what I say will be like a wise man who built his house upon a rock. The rain fell, and the floods came, and the winds blew and beat upon that house, but it did not fall, because it was built on a rock.

"But whoever hears my words but does not do what I say, will be like a foolish man who built his house upon the sand. The rain fell, and the floods came, and the winds blew and beat upon that house, and it fell crashing down."

12 Masses for the Weeks after Pentecost

I

Prayer

Our Father in heaven, send us your Holy Spirit to give us strength and courage to live as true followers of your Son Jesus Christ, our Lord.

Lesson

from the Acts of the Apostles

In those days the apostles worked many miracles among the people. The people as a whole did not dare to join the apostles openly, but they held them in great honour, and more and more of them believed in the Lord Jesus. They brought their sick relations and friends out into the streets so that, when Peter came by, at least his shadow would fall on them, and they would be healed.

Gospel

according to St John

On the last day of the Jewish feast of Tabernacles, Jesus stood up in the Temple and cried: "If anyone is thirsty, let him come to me and drink. He who believes in me, as the Bible says, 'Out of his heart shall flow rivers of living water'." Jesus was talking about the Holy Spirit, which those who believed in him were going to receive. As yet the Spirit had not been given, because Jesus was not yet glorified.

II

Prayer

Father in heaven, send us your Holy Spirit that we may learn to love one another and share with each other all the good things you have given us.

Lesson

from the Acts of the Apostles

In those days all the faithful devoted themselves to the apostles' teaching. They lived together and shared with each other everything they had. If anybody was in need, they sold what they had so that they could help him. Every day they worshipped together in the temple and then went to each other's homes for the breaking of bread. They shared their meals with generous and glad hearts, praising God, and everyone liked them. And every day more and more people joined them.

Gospel

according to St John

At that time Jesus said to the apostles: "Little children I shall only be with you for a little while. Then you will seek me, but you will not be able to go with me to the place where I am going. I am giving you a new commandment. Love one another, as I have loved you. All men will know that you are my disciples if you love one another."

III

Prayer

Almighty Father, make us believe in you with all our hearts, and teach us to love you and everyone else for your sake.

Lesson

from the Acts of the Apostles

In those days Saul was breathing out threats against the disciples of Jesus. He went to the high priest and got permission to go to Damascus. Suddenly a light flashed from heaven, and he fell to the ground, and heard a voice saying to him: "Saul, Saul, why are you persecuting me?" And Saul said: "Who are you, Lord?" And the voice said: "I am Jesus, whom you are persecuting. But get up and go into the city, and you will be told what you have to do."

WEEKS AFTER PENTECOST

Gospel

according to St John

At that time Jesus said to the apostles: "If you do what I tell you, you are my friends. I will not call you servants, for the servant does not know what his master is doing. You are my friends, for I have made known to you all that I have heard from my father. You did not choose me; I chose you, whatever you ask the father in my name, he will give it to you. And this is my commandment to you: You must love one another."

IV

Prayer

Heavenly father, send us your Holy Spirit to make us brave, so that nothing will ever stop us from doing what we know to be your will.

Lesson

from the Acts of the Apostles

Saul stayed for several days with the disciples in Damascus and he at once began preaching in the synagogues, saying: "Jesus is the Son of God." Everyone who heard him was amazed, and said: "Is this not the man who led the attack in Jerusalem against those who call on the name of Jesus? And did he not come here in order to do the same in Damascus?" But Saul grew stronger and stronger, and he put the

Jews to shame by proving that Jesus was the Christ. After a time they plotted to kill him, but Saul got to know about it. They watched the gates of the city night and day, but one night the disciples put Saul in a basket and lowered him over the city wall to safety.

Gospel

according to St John

At that time Jesus said to his disciples: "The world may hate you, but know that it has hated me before it hated you. If you belonged to the world, the world would love you, but it hates you now, because I have chosen you out of the world. Remember what I said to you: 'A servant is not greater than his master.' If they persecuted me, they will persecute you."

V

Prayer

Almighty Father, may your Holy Spirit be with us always, so that we may always be eager to do whatever you want us to do.

Lesson

from the Book of Genesis

The Lord once came to Abram in a vision and said to him: "Fear not, Abram. I am your shield; your

reward will be very great." But Abram said: "O Lord God, what will you give me? Remember I am still childless." And the Lord took him out of doors and said to him: "Look up at the sky, and count the stars, if you can. You will have as many descendants as there are stars in the sky." And Abram believed the Lord and the Lord was pleased with him.

Gospel

according to St Matthew

At that time, as Jesus was walking by the Sea of Galilee, he saw two brothers, Simon who is called Peter, and Andrew. They were casting a net into the sea, for they were fishermen. Jesus said to them: "Follow me, and I will make you fishers of men" At once they left their nets and followed him. Going on from there, Jesus saw two other men, James the son of Zebedee and John his brother. They were sitting in a boat with Zebedee their father, mending their nets. Jesus called them, and at once they left their father in the boat, and followed him.

WEEKS AFTER PENTECOST

VI

Prayer

Almighty and everliving God, king of heaven and earth; listen with kindness to the prayer of your Church, and give peace to the world.

Epistle

from St Paul's letter to the Colossians

Brothers and sisters, love each other with all your hearts. Be kind and humble, gentle and patient. Put up with one another's failings, and forgive one another, as the Lord has forgiven you. And above all have love. Let everything that you do and say be done for the sake of Jesus, the Lord. And through Jesus give thanks to God the Father.

Gospel

according to St Matthew

One day Jesus went with his disciples on board ship. Suddenly a great storm arose and the waves rose high over the ship, but Jesus lay asleep. The disciples came and roused him, saying: "Save us Lord; we are sinking." Jesus said to them: "Why are you afraid, you men of little faith?" Then he rose up and commanded the winds and the sea, and the storm ceased and the sea became calm. His disciples were amazed and said: "What kind of man is this, who is obeyed even by the winds and the sea?"

VII

Prayer

Almighty and everliving God, send us your Holy Spirit to dwell in us as in his holy temple, so that we may always pray to you with all our hearts.

Lesson

from the First Book of Kings

At that time King Solomon dedicated to God the temple he had built. When the priests came out of the holy place, a cloud filled the house of the Lord. Then Solomon stood before the altar of the Lord in the presence of all the people of Israel. He spread out his hands towards heaven, and said: "O Lord, God of Israel, there is no God like you. You give yourself to your people and love all those who serve you with all their hearts. Look upon this house I have built and make it a house of prayer. And always hear the prayers which your people make to you in this temple."

Gospel

according to St John

At that time the feast of the Passover was drawing near, and Jesus went up to Jerusalem. In the temple he found people selling oxen and sheep and pigeons, and the money-changers were sitting at their tables. Jesus made a whip of cords and drove them all with their

WEEKS AFTER PENTECOST

sheep and their oxen out of the temple. And he poured out the coins of the money-changers and overturned their tables. And he told those who sold the pigeons: "Take these things away. My father's house should be a house of prayer, but you have turned it into a den of robbers."

VIII

Prayer

Heavenly Father, may your Holy Spirit make us always to be your loyal, obedient and loving children, so that we may enter one day into your glorious kingdom.

Epistle

from St Paul's first letter to the Corinthians

Brothers and sisters, love is always patient and kind; it is never jealous: love is never boastful or conceited. It is never rude or selfish; it does not take offence, and it is not resentful. It is always ready to excuse, to trust, to hope and to put up with everything that comes.

WEEKS AFTER PENTECOST

Gospel

according to St Mark

At that time Jesus came with his disciples to Capernaum. When he was in the house, he asked them: "What were you talking about on the way?" But they were silent, because on the way they had been arguing about which of them was the greatest. Jesus sat down and said to them "If any of you wants to be first, he must become the last of all and the servant of all." He called a child and made him stand in their midst. Then he took the child in his arms and said to them: "Unless you become like this little child you will never enter the kingdom of heaven. And whoever receives one such child in my name is receiving me; and whoever receives me, receives not me but my Father who sent me."

IX

Prayer

Heavenly Father, let us not put our trust in our own strength, nor in money nor power nor any earthly thing, but only in you and the Holy Spirit that you send to dwell in our hearts.

Lesson

from the Book of Jeremiah, the prophet

Unhappy is the man who puts his trust in man, and who relies on earthly things. His heart is turned away

from the Lord. He is like dry grass in the desert. He is like a man who lives in a land without water, a salt land that is uninhabited. But happy is the man who puts his trust in the Lord. He is like a tree planted by the river. It has nothing to fear when the sun grows hot. Its leaves are always green.

Gospel

according to St Matthew

At that time Jesus said to his disciples: "He who loves father or mother more than me, is not worthy of me; and he who loves son or daughter more than me, is not worthy of me; and he who does not take up his cross and follow me, is not worthy of me.

"For which of you, when he wants to build a tower, does not first sit down and count the cost, asking himself if he has enough material to finish it? Otherwise, when he has started it and cannot finish it everybody will laugh at him saying: 'This man began to build, and was not able to finish.' Or what king, going to war with another king, will not first sit down and ask himself if he is able with ten thousand men to meet him who comes against him with twenty thousand? And if not, while the other is still a great way off he sends an embassy and asks for peace.

"In the same way, anyone who does not give up all he has, cannot be my disciple."

X
Prayer

Almighty Father, Jesus is the true, the living bread come down from heaven. Give us this bread always, so that we may have the strength to make our journey through life and reach your glorious kingdom.

Lesson

from the First Book of Kings

At that time Elijah came to Beer-sheba, a town of Judah, where he left his servant. He himself went on into the desert, a day's journey, and sitting under a furze bush wished he were dead. "Lord", he said, "I have had enough. Take my life; I am no better than my fathers were." Then he lay down and went to sleep. But an angel of the Lord touched him and said: "Get up and eat," He looked round, and there at his head was a scone baked on hot stones, and a jar of water. He ate and drank and then lay down again. But the angel came again and touched him and said: "Get up and eat, or the journey will be too long for you." So he got up and ate and drank, and strengthened by that food he walked for forty days and forty nights, until he reached Horeb, the mountain of God.

Gospel

according to St Mark

When Jesus came to the shore he found a great crowd of people, and he had pity on them, because they were like sheep without a shepherd. And he began to teach them many things. When it grew late his disciples came to him and said: "This is a lonely place and the hour is late; send them away to the villages so that they can buy themselves something to eat." But Jesus said to them: "You give them something to eat." They said: "Shall we go and buy two hundred silver coins' worth of bread?" And Jesus said: "How much bread have you?" When they had found out they said "We have five loaves and two fishes." Then he told the people to sit down in groups on the grass. Taking the five loaves and two fishes, he looked up to heaven and said the blessing. Then he broke the loaves and gave them to the disciples to set before the people. He also divided the two fishes among them. Everyone had enough to eat, and when they had finished the disciples gathered up twelve baskets full of broken pieces and of fish. Those who had eaten the loaves numbered five thousand.

WEEKS AFTER PENTECOST

XI

Prayer

Heavenly Father, teach us to pray with all our hearts, to thank you for loving us so much, and in return to show our love for you and for all your people.

Epistle
from St Paul's letter to the Ephesians

Brothers and sisters, this is what I pray as I kneel down before the Father: may he give you the power of the Spirit so that you may grow strong. May he give you faith, so that Christ may live in your hearts and you may be able to understand how much Christ loves you.

Gospel
according to St Luke

One day Jesus was praying, and when he finished praying one of his disciples said to him: "Lord, teach us to pray, as John the Baptist taught his disciples." And Jesus said to him "When you pray say this: Our father, who art in heaven, hallowed be thy name. Thy kingdom come, thy will be done on earth as it is in heaven. Give us this day our daily bread, and forgive us our trespasses as we forgive those who trespass against us; and lead us not into temptation but deliver us from all evil. If you forgive men the wrong they do you, your heavenly father will also forgive you. But if you do not forgive other people, your father will not forgive you either."

WEEKS AFTER PENTECOST

XII

Prayer

Almighty and everliving God, we look forward to the day when Jesus will come again and change this world into the new heaven and the new earth. Teach us to live for that day, so that while we work in this world our hearts may always be in heaven.

Lesson

from the Apocalypse of St John

Then, I, John saw the holy city, the new Jerusalem, coming down from heaven from God, prepared as a bride ready to meet her husband. I saw no temple in the city, for its temple is the Lord God, the Almighty, and the Lamb. And the city has no need of the sun or the moon to shine on it, for the glory of God is its light, and its lamp is the Lamb.

Gospel

according to St Luke

At that time Jesus said to his disciples: "Fear not, little flock, for it is my Father's wish to give you the Kingdom. Sell what you have and give to the poor; get yourselves purses which do not wear out, treasure that will not fail you, in heaven where no thief can reach it and no moth destroy it. For your heart will be where your treasure is in heaven.

Christ the King

The last Sunday of the year before Advent

Prayer

Almighty and everliving God, you have made Jesus King of all the world. Have mercy on us all, and bring all men under his gentle rule. He lives and reigns with you and the Holy Spirit, one God, for ever and ever.

Epistle

from St Paul's letter to the Colossians

Brothers and sisters, we give thanks to God our Father for rescuing us from the power of darkness, and bringing us into the Kingdom of his Son. Christ has ransomed us with his blood and forgiven us our sins. He is the head of the Church.

Gospel
according to St Matthew

At that time Pilate said to Jesus: "Are you king of the Jews?" Jesus answered: "Do you say this of your own accord, or is it what others have told you of me?" Pilate said: "Am I a Jew? It is your own nation and its chief priests who have given you up to me. What have you done wrong?" Jesus answered: "My kingdom does not belong to this world. If my kingdom were one which belonged to this world, my servants would be fighting to prevent my falling into the hands of the Jews. But my kingdom is not an earthly kingdom." Then Pilate said: "You are a king then?" And Jesus answered: "As you say, I am a king. But the reason why I was born and came into the world was to teach men the truth. My followers are those who belong to the truth."

Immaculate Conception
8 December

Prayer

O God, you kept Mary free from every trace of sin, from the very first moment when she began to live in her mother's womb. You did this because she was to be the Mother of Jesus, and you knew that Jesus would die for her as he died for us. She is praying for us now. Hear her prayers, and make us sinless too.

Lesson
from the Book of Proverbs

God made me his own before the world began;

long, long ago, before he made the earth, the rivers and the sea. God was all my joy, and I loved to be with the children of men. Listen, then, to me, you who are my children. Do as I say, and you will find happiness. Listen to my teaching, and you will be wise. To find me is to find life, for the Lord will save you.

Gospel

according to St Luke

At that time God sent the angel Gabriel to a city of Galilee called Nazareth. Mary was living there, a young maiden, engaged to be married to Joseph, who belonged to the family of David. The angel went to her and said: "Hail, full of grace; the Lord is with thee; blessed art thou among women."

Presentation of the Lord

Candlemas

2 February

Prayer

Almighty and everliving God, today the infant Jesus was taken by his mother to the temple. When we come to church make us pure and holy as he was.

Lesson

from the Book of Malachi, the Prophet

This is what the Lord says: "See, I am sending my angel to prepare the way for the Lord for whom you are waiting. See, he is coming! He will purify you, as gold and silver are purified by fire. Then once more the Lord will accept your offerings."

Gospel

according to St Luke

When the time had come for Mary's purification according to the law of Moses, Mary and Joseph brought Jesus to Jerusalem to present him to the Lord.

At this time there was a man named Simeon living in Jerusalem, an upright, God-fearing man, who was waiting patiently for Israel's redeemer. Led by the

Holy Spirit, he now came into the Temple, and when Jesus was brought in by his parents, he took the Child in his arms and said: "Now, Lord, you may send your servant away in peace, for my own eyes have seen your saving power. This is the light which all the nations will see; this is the glory of your own people, Israel."

Joseph the Worker

1 May

Prayer

O God, you made all things, and you have told men that they must work too. May St Joseph help us by his example and his prayers to do our work properly, for you have promised us a great reward if we work well.

Epistle

from St Paul's letter to the Colossians

Brothers and sisters, love one another, and you will all be united together. Your hearts must be full of that peace which Christ alone can give you. He wants you to have peace; that is why he has called you to be Christians. And you must learn to be grateful. Work hard; and remind yourselves that it is for the Lord that you are working, not for men. Christ is your Master.

Gospel
according to St Matthew

At that time Jesus came to his own country, and he taught the people in their place of worship, the synagogue. The people were very surprised, and said: "How did he come by this wisdom and these strange powers? Is not this the carpenter's son, whose mother is called Mary. Where did he get all this power?" They could not believe that he was genuine. But Jesus said to them: "It is only in his own country and in his own house that a prophet is without honour." Jesus did not work many miracles there, because the people would not believe in him.

Birth of John the Baptist
24 June

Prayer

O God, you have given us this day on which we honour the birth of St John the Baptist. Make all your people happy, and help us all to get to heaven.

Lesson

from the Book of Isaiah, the Prophet

The Lord chose me to be his prophet even before I

was born. His words sank deep into my heart. He kept me safe, and he said to me: "You are my servant. You will be the light of the heathen nations. You must preach the message of salvation to the farthest corners of the earth. When they see you, kings and princes will fall down and worship the Lord."

Gospel

according to St Luke

Elizabeth gave birth to a son, and her friends and relations, hearing the news, came to congratulate her. On the eighth day after his birth the child had to be circumcised, and they wanted to give him the name Zachary, because that was his father's name. But his mother said: "No, he is to be called John." "But," they said, "none of your relations has that name;" and they made signs to his father asking him what name he wanted to give him. Zachary, who was dumb, called for a writing-tablet and on it he wrote the words: "His name is John". Everyone was surprised. In that instant Zachary found that he could speak again, and at once he began to praise God. When the news of what had happened spread throughout the countryside, the people were astonished and said: "Why then, what will this boy grow to be? For indeed the hand of the Lord is upon him."

Then his father Zachary was filled with the Holy Spirit, and he said: "Blessed be the Lord, the God of Israel; he has visited his people and brought them redemption."

Peter and Paul, Apostles

29 June

Prayer

O God, you have made this day holy by the martyrdom of your apostles Peter and Paul. May we always follow their teaching, and remain true to the faith which they have given us.

Lesson

from the Acts of the Apostles

In those days Herod used his power to hunt down some of the leading Christians. He beheaded James, the brother of John, and seeing that this pleased the Jews, he went further and laid hands on Peter too. He put him in prison, and had him closely guarded. But the Church prayed for him all the time. The night before he was to be brought out for trial, Peter was asleep chained between two soldiers, and there were sentries at the door guarding his prison. Suddenly an angel of the Lord stood over him, and a light shone in

his cell. The angel woke Peter up and said to him: "Quick, rise up." The chains fell from his hands, and the angel said: "Put your cloak on and follow me." Thinking that he was dreaming, Peter followed the angel. The door stood open, and they went out. When they were out in the street the angel left him. Then Peter said: "Now I know for sure that the Lord has sent his angel to rescue me from Herod's power."

Gospel

according to St Matthew

One day Jesus asked his disciples: "Who do people think I am?" They answered: "Some think you are John the Baptist, others Elijah, or Jeremiah, or one of the other prophets." Then Jesus said to them: "But who do you think I am?" And Peter answered: "You are the Christ, the Son of the living God." Jesus replied: "You are blessed indeed, Simon, for no man has told you this; you have it from my Father in heaven. And I tell you this: you are Peter, the rock on which I will build my Church, and hell itself will never be able to conquer it. I will give you the keys of the kingdom of heaven. Whatever you shall bind on earth shall be bound in heaven, and whatever you shall loose on earth shall be loosed in heaven."

Transfiguration

6 August

Prayer

O God, the apostles have told us how you strengthened their faith by showing them Jesus in his glory, and by speaking to them from a shining cloud. You have strengthened our faith too. May we live forever with Jesus, our King, in his glory in heaven.

Epistle

from St Peter's second letter

My dear friends, we have actually seen the power and glory of our Lord Jesus Christ. Such honour, such glory was given him by God the Father, that a voice came to him out of a shining cloud, saying: "This is my beloved Son in whom I am well pleased; you must

TRANSFIGURATION

listen to him." We heard this voice coming from heaven when we were with him on the holy mountain.

Gospel

according to St Matthew

At that time Jesus took Peter, James and John up onto a high mountain.

There his whole appearance was changed as they looked at him. His face shone like the sun, his garments became white as snow. Moses and Elijah appeared at his side, speaking with him.

Peter said: "Lord, it is good for us to be here. Let us build three dwellings here, one for you, one for Moses, and one for Elijah." While he was speaking, a shining cloud overshadowed them, and a voice spoke from the cloud: "This is my beloved Son in whom I am well pleased; you must listen to him." The apostles fell on their faces in fear, but Jesus came and touched them, saying: "Stand up; do not be afraid." They lifted up their eyes and saw no one there but Jesus. As they came down from the mountain Jesus said to them: "Do not tell anyone what you have seen until I have risen from the dead."

Assumption

Mary is taken up into heaven
15 August

Prayer

Almighty and everliving God, you have taken up the sinless virgin Mary, the mother of your Son, body and soul into heaven. Help us to live as we should, so that one day we may share with her the happiness of heaven.

Lesson

from the Book of Judith

The Lord has blessed you with his own power. You are more blessed than every other woman in the world. Praised be God, the maker of heaven and earth, for sending you to strike down our great enemy. Such fame has he given you this day, that men will never cease to praise you, so long as they remember what the Lord had done for them.

Gospel

according to St Luke

At that time Mary rose up and went with all haste to a town of Juda, in the hill-country where Zachary lived.

GUARDIAN ANGELS

She entered his house and greeted Elizabeth. As soon as Elizabeth heard Mary's greeting, the child in her womb leaped for joy, and Elizabeth herself was filled with the Holy Spirit. "Blessed art thou among women," she said, "and blessed is the fruit of thy womb. How have I deserved to be visited by the mother of my Lord? Why, as soon as I heard your greeting, the child in my womb leaped for joy."

Then Mary said:

> "My soul glorifies the Lord,
> my spirit rejoices in God, my Saviour.
> He looks on his servant in her nothingness;
> henceforth all ages will call me blessed.
> The almighty works marvels for me;
> holy is his name.
> His mercy is from age to age
> on those who fear him."

Guardian Angels

2 October

Prayer

O God, we thank you for sending your holy angels to keep watch over us, and we look forward to sharing

their happiness for ever in heaven. Give us this grace through your Son, Jesus Christ our Lord.

Lesson

from the Book of Exodus

This is what the Lord says: "I am sending out an angel of mine to go before you, and to take care of you wherever you go. Pay attention to him, and listen to his voice. If you take note of what he says and do whatever I tell you, I will keep you safe from your enemies, and my angel will always be at your side."

Gospel

according to St Matthew

One day the disciples came to Jesus and said: "Tell us, who is the greatest in the kingdom of heaven?" Jesus called a little child to his side and said: "Believe me, unless you become like a little child, you shall never enter the kingdom of heaven. The greatest person in the kingdom of heaven is the person who humbles himself like this little child. And anyone who cares for a child like this for my sake is caring for me. But if anyone leads one of these little ones of mine into sin, it would be better for him to be drowned in the depths of the sea, with a millstone round his neck. See to it that you do not treat one of these little ones with contempt; I tell you they have angels in heaven, who forever gaze upon my Father's face."

All Saints
1 November

Prayer

Almighty and everliving God, we have many friends in heaven who are praying for us on this feast day of all your saints. Hear their prayers, and look on us with kindness.

Lesson

from the Apocalypse of St John

At that time I saw another angel coming from the east. He cried out with a loud voice to the four angels who had been given power to destroy the land and sea saying: "Do not destroy the land and sea until we have put a sign on the foreheads of those who serve our God." And I saw thousands and thousands of saints standing before God's throne in the presence of the Lamb. They were dressed in white, and held palm-branches in their hands. They cried out with a loud voice: "All glory be to God, who sits on the throne, and to the Lamb." And all the angels were standing round the throne. They fell on their faces and worshipped God, saying: "To our God be all glory and wisdom and thanks and honour and power and strength for ever and ever. Amen."

Gospel
according to St Matthew

At that time, when Jesus saw how great the crowd was, he went up on to the mountainside. There he sat down and his disciples came to him. And he said to them: "Blessed are the poor in spirit; the kingdom of heaven is theirs."

Blessed are the patient; they shall reach the promised land.

Blessed are those who mourn; they shall be comforted.

Blessed are those who hunger and thirst for holiness; they shall have their heart's desire.

Blessed are the merciful; they shall receive mercy.

Blessed are the clean of heart; they shall see God.

Blessed are those who spread peace about them; they shall be called God's children.

Blessed are you when men blame you, and bully you, and tell wicked lies about you because of me. Be glad and rejoice, for a rich reward is waiting for you in heaven."

All Souls

2 November　　　　　　　The Mass for the Dead

Prayer

O God, creator and redeemer of all the faithful, forgive the sins of all your people whose life on earth is ended. Give them eternal life; for you are God, who lives and reigns for ever and ever.

Epistle

from St Paul's letter to the Corinthians

Brothers and sisters, here is a secret I will make known to you: we shall all rise again from the grave. It will happen in a moment, in the twinkling of an eye, when the last trumpet sounds. The dead will be raised up to life again. Our bodies will never die any more; they will be immortal. What the Bible says will come true: "Where, death, is your victory?" Let us thank God, who gives us victory through our Lord Jesus Christ.

Gospel

according to St John

At that time Jesus said to the Jews: "The time is coming when the dead will hear the voice of the Son of God, and those who hear it will live. All those who are in their graves will hear his voice, and will come out of them. Those whose actions have been good will rise to new life; and those whose actions have been wicked will rise to meet their judgment."

For Feasts of our Lord

Prayer

O God, our Father, you sent us your Son, Jesus Christ our Lord. He died for us on the cross, and rose again to give us his own divine life. We long to be with him in his glory in heaven.

Epistle
from St Paul's letter to the Philippians

Brothers and sisters, you must be like Jesus Christ. Even though he is God, he did not cling to the magnificence that is his due as God. He laid it all aside and became a man, just like every other man. He became humble and obedient, even to the point of accepting death—even on a cross.

That is why God has raised him to such a height, and given him a name that is greater than any other name. At the name of Jesus everyone in heaven and on earth must kneel; everyone must proclaim that the Lord Jesus Christ dwells in the glory of God the Father.

Gospel
according to St John

Jesus once said to Nicodemus: "God loves the world so much that he sent his only Son into it, and those who believe in him will not be lost, but will live for ever." God did not send his Son into the world as its judge, but as its saviour.

For Feasts of our Lady

Prayer

O God, our Father, we love to celebrate the feasts of Mary, the mother of Jesus, and our own mother too. Hear her prayers for us. Keep us safe from all danger, and make us live with you for ever in heaven.

Lesson

from the Book of Ecclesiasticus

Before the world was made, God made me, and I shall live for ever and ever. I was his servant in his holy dwelling-place, and now Jerusalem, God's holy city, is my home. I am queen in Jerusalem, queen over the people whom God loves. God has given me a share in his own kingdom, and I love to be with his holy people.

Gospel

according to St Luke

At that time God sent the angel Gabriel to a maiden who was living in the town of Nazareth, in Galilee. Her name was Mary. The angel said to her: "Do not be afraid, Mary, God loves you. You are going to have a son, and you must call him Jesus. He will be great, and men will know him for the Son of the most High. The Lord God will give him the throne of his Father, David, and he will rule over the house of Jacob for

FEASTS OF APOSTLES

ever. His kingdom will never end." And Mary said: "Behold the handmaid of the Lord; be it done to me according to your word."

For Feasts of Apostles

Prayer

O God, our Father, make your people holy and keep them safe. Hear the prayers of your holy apostle, and help us to live as you want us to live, and to serve you in peace.

Epistle

from St Paul's letter to the Romans

Brothers and sisters, the Bible says: "Everyone who calls on the name of the Lord will be saved." But how can anyone call on the Lord's name before he has learned to believe? And how can anyone learn to believe in the Lord, if he has never heard of him? And how will he ever get to hear of him, unless someone is sent to teach him about the Lord? That is why the Bible says: "How welcome are those who come bringing the good news."

Gospel

according to St Matthew

Jesus once said to his apostles: "All power has been given to me in heaven and on earth. Go, therefore, and make disciples of all nations, and baptize them in the name of the Father, and of the Son and of the Holy Ghost. You must teach them to keep all the commandments I have given you. Behold, I am with you all through the days that are coming, until the end of the world."

For the Feast of a Martyr
Prayer

Almighty God, hear the prayers of your martyr. Help us to love you as much as he did, and to be strong and faithful, even when things are difficult.

Epistle
from St Paul's letter to Timothy

Dear friend, keep you mind fixed on Jesus Christ, who has risen from the dead; that is the gospel I preach, and because I preach it I am treated like a criminal, and kept in prison. But the word of God cannot be imprisoned. I am ready to suffer anything at all, so that men may be saved through Jesus Christ, and live for ever in the glory of heaven.

I have had to suffer many hardships, but the Lord brought me through them all safely. Everyone who lives as Jesus wants him to will have to suffer hardships.

Gospel
according to St Matthew

One day Jesus said to his disciples: "Those who want

to be my disciples must take up their cross every day and follow me. Those who cling to life will lose it; but those who give up their lives for my sake will find new life. What is the use of gaining the whole world, if in doing so you lose your soul?"

For the Feast of a Saint

Prayer

O God, we love to celebrate this yearly feastday of your saint. Help us to love you as much as he did, and to live as you want us to live.

Lesson

from the Book of Ecclesiasticus

Happy is the man who was without sin, and who was not led astray by the desire for gold and riches. He is the man we will praise; he is the man whose life we admire. The perfect man has earned unending fame. He could have sinned, but he did not sin; he could have done wrong, but he did no wrong. The good that he did will never be forgotten. The whole Church will speak of his kindness and generosity.

Gospel

according to St Luke

Jesus once said to his disciples: "Do not be afraid, my little flock. Your Father is going to give you his kingdom. Sell what you have, so as to help the poor. Your treasure will then be kept in a purse which will never wear out. It will be a heavenly treasure, which no thief can take from you. If your treasure is in heaven, your heart will be there too."

For the Feast of a Holy Woman

Prayer

Hear us, O God our Saviour. As we celebrate this feast day of your saint, teach us to give ourselves to you with childlike love.

Epistle
from St Paul's letter to the Corinthians

Brothers and sisters, no one has any right to boast of his own merits, but only of what Christ has done through him. Listen, then, to the boast I am going to make. I am jealous for you with a jealousy that comes from God. I have made you Christ's bride so that no one but he shall claim you, his bride without stain.

Gospel
according to St Matthew

One day Jesus told his disciples the following parable: "The kingdom of heaven is like a treasure, buried in a field. Someone found it and, rejoicing in his good fortune, he went off home and sold all he had, so as to be able to buy that field.

"Again, the kingdom of heaven is as if a trader were looking for rare pearls. And now he has found one pearl of great cost, and has sold all that he had and bought it.

"The kingdom of heaven is like a net that was cast into the sea. When the net was full of fish, the fishermen drew it up, and sat down on the beach, where they sorted out the good fish from the useless fish. They put the good fish in their buckets, and threw the useless fish back into the sea. That is what will happen at the end of the world."

Index of Seasons and Feasts

Season of Advent

First week 60
Second week 62
Third week 63
Fourth week 65

Christmas Season

Christmas: Midnight Mass 66
Christmas: Mass during the day 69
Sunday in the Octave of Christmas: Holy Family 70
6 January: Epiphany 72

Lenten Season

Ash Wednesday 74
First week of Lent 75
Second week of Lent 77
Third week of Lent 79
Fourth week of Lent 80
Fifth week of Lent 82
Passion Sunday (Palm Sunday) 83

Easter Triduum and Easter Season

Holy Thursday 85
Good Friday: a play for Good Friday 88
    Holy communion on Good Friday 95
Easter Vigil: Holy Saturday 96
Easter Sunday 99
Second week of Easter 100
Third week of Easter 102
Fourth week of Easter 103
Fifth week of Easter 105
Ascension 106
Pentecost 108

Solemnities of the Lord during the Season of the Year

Trinity Sunday 110
The Body and Blood of the Lord (Corpus Christi) 111
The Sacred Heart of Jesus 112

The Season of the Year

Six Masses for the weeks after Epiphany 114
Twelve Masses for the weeks after Pentecost 121
Christ the King (Last Sunday of the Year) 136

Masses of the Saints

Immaculate Conception (8 December) 137
Presentation of the Lord (2 February) 139
Joseph the Worker (1 May) 140
Birth of John the Baptist (24 June) 141
Peter and Paul, Apostles (29 June) 143
Transfiguration (6 August) 145
Assumption (15 August) 147
Guardian Angels (2 October) 148
All Saints (1 November) 150
All Souls (2 Novemeber) 152
For feasts of our Lord 153
For feasts of our Lady 154
For feasts of apostles 155
For the feast of a martyr 156
For the feast of a saint 157
For the feast of a holy woman 158